From Gloria Lancaster

Xmas 1971

BABA

ARNOLD SCHULMAN

BABA

NEW YORK / THE VIKING PRESS

TO LISA

LIST OF ILLUSTRATIONS

BABA

✿ ONE

The village of Puttaparthi, which does not appear on any map, can be found in the southern part of India one hundred and twenty-seven miles north of Bangalore. Physically, it is a handful of mud huts, perhaps twenty or thirty, clustered in no particular order at the foot of two dwarfed hills of rock surrounded by a parched and desolate wasteland of red clay dust. Technologically, it is about ten minutes past the Stone Age.

Shortly after noon when the writer, an American, arrived in a ten-year-old taxi from Bangalore, it was a hundred and twenty in the shade. The only sign of life in any direction was a mangy dog having a fit.

The trip had taken more than five hours, starting on a well-paved, two-lane highway; but the farther the writer and the driver got from Bangalore the narrower the road became until finally there was no road at all. For the last nine miles the car had bounced recklessly over dusty hills and fields. Twice it had to inch across shallow creeks.

As the driver unloaded the five suitcases strapped to the top of the car, the writer took his tape recorder, camera bag, and portable typewriter from the back seat. Ordinarily, he traveled with as little baggage as possible, but having been to India once before he had prepared for almost any emergency.

He had come to India the first time to research a film he planned to write. He had been in love with India then—not with India as it was but as he had imagined it should be— and like many disillusioned lovers, when the infatuation ended he had felt betrayed.

From the first moment he arrived in Bombay it was as if he had suddenly plunged through the barriers of time and space onto another planet in another century. He felt bewildered, disoriented, on the edge of panic. Perhaps there was too much reality, or maybe it was of a different kind. Whatever it was, he found the network of his emotions malfunctioning like a badly programed computer. The more he tried to clutch at some recognizable frame of reference, the more he felt like a man on the edge of madness stumbling through the fifth dimension of a surrealistic nightmare he could neither digest nor comprehend. All he knew was that something in the air, he couldn't define what, had penetrated almost immediately beneath the level of his senses to attack what he reluctantly conceded might be his soul.

He knew very little about the geography of his soul. He had accepted the Hindu idea that he was not his body. Neither was he his mind. But the basic question, of course, was who exactly was the "he" who could or could not accept anything, and he was still working on that one.

In truth he considered himself something of a closet mystic, being somewhat more involved than a fad-rider but far less dedicated than a full-time seeker. Born Jewish, he still identified with his Jewishness, but on the level of enjoying a piece of gefüllte fish now and then. Theologically, he could never accept the idea that God was some super deal-maker in the sky.

When he was in his early twenties (nearly fifteen years before the incidents covered in this account), he had come across a book on Zen and the concept of man being entirely responsible for his own destiny immediately appealed to his sense of logic. He read everything on the subject he could find—in spite of the orthodox Freudian analyst he was going to at the time who objected so strongly that she broke her customary silence to suggest that his interest in Zen was nothing more than another form of resistance.

At the first opportunity the writer went to Japan.

To his astonishment his first attempts at meditation were torturous. (Before he tried it, the idea of sitting on the floor without moving a muscle or thinking a single thought seemed an easy enough thing to do.) After only a few seconds both legs went to sleep, his nose itched, and a pain in the middle of his back quickly became excruciating. In less than five minutes he gave up.

The next day he tried again with even less success, but he doggedly continued to practice, even after he returned to New York, all the while being careful to assure himself that none of this had anything to do with religion. The word "religion" was infested with too many connotations he found impossible to accept. He was a writer, he rationalized, and his mind was the principal tool of his craft. Therefore, it was imperative that he learn to control it. Just as a pianist needed exercises to develop command of his fingers, he needed a systematic series of études for his brain. So, under the license of pragmatism, his conscience allowed him to continue practicing meditation until, over a period of several years, he progressed to where he could sit in the full lotus position for more than an hour at a time—his body completely motionless, his mind almost completely blank.

His work improved and so did his income, first as a playwright, then as a film writer. He married an actress, moved from a basement in Greenwich Village to Sutton Place South, and in time had two children, a boy and girl. For Christmas they went to Saint-Moritz. Summers were spent in the South of France. The children went to a private school where the classes were conducted entirely in French which made it necessary to have a French governess (in addition to the cook, laundress, and housekeeper) to help the children with their homework.

Hardly the life of an ascetic, but meanwhile he had been accepted as a student and given a koan by Miura Roshi, a Zen Master who in the genealogical charts of Zen lines was the direct descendant of Bodhidharma, the Indian saint who brought Zen to China in the sixth century.

For several years the writer struggled to find the answer to the unanswerable riddle of the koan. Eventually, having made no apparent progress, he gave up, saving what little face he could by telling himself that he wasn't actually giving up. He was just relegating the job of solving the koan to his unconscious, and, when he least expected it, the answer would suddenly pop into his head. It didn't fool his unconscious, though, any more than it fooled his conscience, or for that matter, the koan.

One day, while filling out a routine questionnaire from his children's school, he found himself writing the word "Buddhist" in the blank where he was supposed to state their religion. He was surprised and a little unnerved to discover what he had written. When he was a child, he had always declared on questionnaires that he was "Hebrew," a word that in the South, where he grew up, seemed somehow less Jewish. But once he moved to New York and discovered it was considered chic in certain groups, he frequently found himself flaunting what he now called his cultural heritage (as differentiated from religion) with a belligerence he usually mistook for pride. But now Buddhist?

Since the word "Buddhist" had come directly from his unconscious, it occurred to him that perhaps he had really meant it; there was also the possibility that he had merely acquired another affectation to dangle as a badge of eccentricity. This was a conclusion he found so painful he immediately assumed it was true.

He continued working with Miura Roshi but, at the same time, began taking instructions from first one yogi then another, eclectically adding a few basic yoga postures and breathing exercises to the meditation which by now had become as integral a part of his life as eating and sleeping.

Philosophically, Roshi stressed the total absence of mysticism, promising rewards only in exact proportion to the amount of effort spent. The logic of this approach continued to satisfy his intellect, but the child in him longed for a Father who lived in Heaven. Unfortunately, the concept of God as worshiped by conventional religions in the West seemed too symbolic. He looked for conclusive evidence to establish that Jesus Christ had actually lived on this earth but he found none. Only what he read about the great Indian sages, saints, and yogis seemed to satisfy his need for a superhuman Father without violating his sense of plausibility. The yogis were human beings one could see and touch, but (if one could believe the literature about them), as had Christ, they could walk on water, leave their bodies, take loaves of bread from the air, and, above all, offer eternal love, protection, and comfort to their disciples, even after death.

It was the search for such a holy man that had brought the writer back to India, less than a year after swearing to himself that he never wanted to see, hear, talk, or think about that whore of a country again.

The name of the holy man was Sathya Sai Baba who, according to reports, had been performing dozens of miracles every day for nearly thirty years. He was widely known in India. Whenever he made a public appearance it was not unusual for one-hundred-and-fifty-thousand people to show up, many of them having to travel for days on foot to hear him speak. He was said to be able to cure the uncurable, frequently by materializing a handful of ashes in his palm and then rubbing the ashes onto the afflicted part of the body. He could also materialize necklaces, bracelets, rings, photographs, anything a person wanted. It was said he knew everything about anyone who came to see him, including intimate details of their past and specific facts of the future.

The writer heard of Baba during his first stay in India and through a friend, an Indian novelist, had arranged to meet him.

Baba, in his early forties, was slightly over five feet tall. He wore a bright orange silk dress that hung loosely down to his chunky bare feet; but the first thing one noticed was his Afro-electric hair standing straight out from all parts of his head like a black, kinky halo five or six inches wide. His coloring was the soft beige of a Brahmin. He spoke gently and with great sweetness to each of the seven people in the room, but did not reveal anything about anyone's past or future. He confined his remarks to platitudes about God, love, and devotion. Then, just before Baba ended the audience, he materialized a ruby ring, which he gave to the novelist, and a handful of ashes, which he gave to a woman in the group. Baba was talking to someone else on the other side of the room when suddenly he had stopped in the middle of a sentence and turned to the woman.

"I will cure your appendicitis," he said, as he materialized the ashes. "Take this in water three days."

She had suffered an attack of appendicitis the night before and was in great pain. No one had mentioned her attack.

She followed his instructions and three days later, when

the pain had completely disappeared, she had two reputable doctors in another town examine her thoroughly. Neither of them could find any trace of appendicitis.

The writer was not particularly impressed. It was only later, when he tried to reconstruct what he had seen, that he began to wonder if he really had been witness to something extraordinary. Knowing how easy it is for any competent stage illusionist to seem to make all kinds of objects appear and disappear by the careful use of tricks of distraction, the writer had watched Baba carefully as he materialized the ring and the ashes.

First Baba had pushed the sleeve on his right arm up above the elbow, then he held out his empty right hand, palm up. Slowly, casually, he turned his hand palm down and held it motionless a few seconds. His fingers were apart. Nothing could possibly have been concealed between them. Baba was seated in the middle of the floor with the others also seated on the floor in a semicircle around him. The writer was sitting a few inches from Baba's right hand. Knowing it might be considered rude, he nevertheless bent forward to examine Baba's hand as he turned it palm downward. There was nothing hidden between his thumb and the fold of his hand. Nothing was concealed in his palm. Then Baba slowly closed his fingers and turned his hand over at the same time. In one continuous motion he opened his fingers, revealing the ring the first time, the ashes the second time.

What puzzled the writer each time he recalled the incident was the fact that neither he nor anyone else in the room had reacted with surprise, delight, or amazement at what they had seen. Baba had materialized the objects so effortlessly, with so little importance attached to it, that they had accepted what he had done as casually as if he had scratched his head or coughed. Neither had they questioned how Baba could have known about the attack of appendicitis.

The writer returned to New York and his familiar world of mouth wash and deodorants. He had seen the religious fanatics in Benares, the Holy City, and had dismissed them along with the entire Hindu master-disciple relationship as, at best, the sentimental dependency of neurotics, at worst, the systematic exploitation of psychopathic compulsives.

One day, for no reason he could discover, he realized that he had somehow developed a compulsion of his own. He tried to deny it, suppress it, and finally rationalize it, but it wouldn't leave him alone. He had to face it. Something inside of him (he refused to accept the possibility that it might be something outside of him) demanded that he write a book about Sai Baba.

There were any number of reasons why he should not. First of all it would mean having to give up a hundred-and-fifty-thousand-dollar assignment to adapt a screenplay from a novel he genuinely liked. He would have to go back to India, a country he feared and despised. It would mean leaving his family for an extended period of time. But worst of all, it would mean that he had not given up his search for a Master.

A man may search the entire world for his Master, a sage had written, but not until the time was right could he find Him. But when the pupil was ready the Teacher would do the calling and nothing the student could do could prevent his Master from drawing him to his spiritual home. Distance, lack of money, business and family ties—all of these would be resolved in a seemingly logical, effortless way.

As a test the writer sought out a publisher and described the kind of book he wanted to write. It was accepted immediately. Now, all he had to do was clear it with Baba.

He wrote to Dr. V. K. Gokok, vice chancellor of the University of Bangalore, who had arranged for the writer and his friend, the Indian novelist, to meet Baba. Gokok, about sixty, was well over six feet tall. He was heavy and round shouldered, gentle and warm. His thick, horn-rimmed glasses made him resemble a giant, lumbering, benevolent owl.

What the writer wanted was for Gokok to get Baba to agree to allow the writer to spend every minute with him, day and night, for a substantial period of time; to record as many interviews as necessary with Baba, his family, devotees and enemies; and to be present at the interviews Baba had with those who came to him for help. The purpose was to document an ordinary day in Baba's life, on tape, as a witness, and in photographs.

Gokok answered at once. He thought the idea of the book was excellent, and suggested the writer might find it useful to accompany Baba on a tour he was planning through the villages of Andhra Pradesh at the end of January. The writer agreed and Gokok wrote that he would speak to Baba at the first opportunity.

A week before the writer had to leave, in order to get to India in time for the tour, he still had not received Baba's permission. In letter after letter, though, Gokok had reiterated that he felt certain Baba would not object, so the writer continued making preparations for the trip. He booked passage and began carefully accumulating what he later realized was a ludicrous assortment of supplies. Not the least ridiculous were two different kinds of snake-bite kits, each for a different kind of snake.

The writer had met Baba in what was by Indian standards a palatial home in the suburbs of Bangalore, but in Gokok's letters frequent mention was made of a place called Puttaparthi—suggesting that this is where the writer would spend most of his time after the tour. No one the writer questioned in New York had ever heard of Puttaparthi. Not Air India, not members of the Indian Delegation to the UN. Nobody.

The more the writer tried to imagine what lay in store for

him, the more anxious he became and the more supplies he decided were absolutely essential for basic survival.

Finally, after a number of urgent telegrams and garbled telephone conversations from New York to Bangalore (by way of Australia), the writer received a letter from Gokok stating that Baba had given permission for the writer to go with him on the tour and to stay with him as long as the writer thought necessary. He could take as many photographs as he liked, and tape as many interviews as he needed.

At the last moment, the Indian government refused to grant the writer a visa. A tourist's application was automatically processed within twenty-four hours but a writer required careful investigation first. This was not to be misconstrued as having anything to do with censorship, the authorities were quick to point out; they just wanted to prevent unfavorable stories about their country from being written.

How long might it reasonably be expected to take, the writer asked?

Possibly months, he was told.

Since he had so little time and considered it most important to make the tour with Baba, the writer contacted several high-ranking government officials he had met in New Delhi and with their help managed to get the necessary papers only hours before he was scheduled to leave.

Two days before Baba was supposed to begin his tour the writer arrived in Bangalore, exhausted from the thirty-five-hour trip but eager to begin.

Gokok seemed genuinely glad to see him, and as they embraced, warmly and spontaneously, the writer felt a disarmingly unconcealed feeling of love and brotherhood.

That night after an elaborate feast, Indian style, at Gokok's house the six-feet-four host and his five-feet-four guest wandered peacefully in the garden around Gokok's enormous but crumbling house which belonged to the university. Almost no private citizen could afford to live on that scale any more. Thousands of tiny parrots were flying from one gigantic banyan tree to another.

"Every night they do that," Gokok explained. "The same time every night. I don't know why."

The house was on the high ground and from the garden they could see the sun, rich and orange, seeming to rest on the horizon while, at the same time, on the opposite horizon an equally orange moon seemed afloat on the edge of the sky. Together they seemed like a matched pair of electric tangerines, and combined with the ceremony of the parrots, created a strange mood of tranquillity that seemed not entirely of this earth.

Neither Gokok nor the writer spoke for a time and then Gokok quietly began talking of Baba. For many years Gokok had been a disciple of Sri Aurobindo, one of India's most celebrated saints, but due to an accumulation of circumstances and a series of what seemed to be startling coincidences (many having to do with a personal tragedy in Gokok's life), he came to consider himself one of Baba's devotees. The telling of this story was obviously a painful act of generosity, and the writer was moved.

Then Gokok revealed a piece of information which he might not have spoken of if the bond between them had not grown so quickly and so full.

"Baba is an avatar," Gokok said. "An incarnation of God, you know. He said so."

For a moment the writer just looked at him. In no way could he justify such a statement coming from an educated, rational, thoroughly respected, highly Westernized man like Gokok. The writer had accepted the supposition that Baba was, indeed, able to perform the seemingly miraculous feats he was famous for; but this acceptance was based on the logical assumption that Baba accomplished all this through the skillful use of his highly developed powers of yoga. That was the biggest assumption the writer was prepared to accept.

Gokok noticed the writer's reaction and laughed.

"I know," he said. "For a man to say such a thing he must either be mad or else . . ." He hesitated, tried to smile to conceal the depth of his feeling, ". . . or else He is God."

A third alternative immediately occurred to the writer: Suppose Baba were neither mad nor God but simply a very talented charlatan cleverly utilizing the Indian readiness to accept the idea of living avatars? Throughout the history of India there have always been men who claimed to be avatars, and while each of them managed to accumulate a sizable following in India, the same man making the same statements in America could very easily have found himself in a mental institution. It is part of the Indian nature to accept the occult, just as in America it is considered normal to be suspicious.

They walked around to the front of the house where a car was waiting to take the writer back to his hotel, but as the chauffeur got out and opened the door Gokok suddenly remembered something.

"One minute," he said, and rushed into the house. On a table near the door in the enormous reception room Gokok found a book he obviously had placed there earlier in the evening so he wouldn't forget it. It was a biography of Baba written by a man in his seventies who had spent the last twenty years living with Baba, worshiping him.

"You might find this interesting," Gokok said. "At least as a beginning."

Baba had arrived in Bangalore that day as scheduled and was having dinner that night with the governor. The next night Gokok was supposed to take the writer to Baba's house in Whitefield, the suburb where the writer had met Baba the time before.

After having dinner with Baba the writer would spend the night there and early the next morning they would begin the tour.

"He's expecting me, isn't he?" the writer had asked.

"Of course. Everything is taken care of. We leave everything to Baba now."

The next night when they arrived at Whitefield they discovered that Baba had left about three o'clock that afternoon.

Gokok was baffled. He had been told specifically to be there at seven, not only to introduce the writer but also to discuss some urgent business in connection with the college Baba wanted to begin in Bangalore.

"Did he say anything?" Gokok asked the caretaker, a mild and beaming little man in his seventies.

"He just said, 'Let's go, we're leaving,'" the caretaker reported. "You know how he does. And they left."

"At three o'clock?"

"Two, three o'clock," the caretaker said.

Gokok and the caretaker laughed. They were used to Baba's inexplicable behavior and enjoyed it.

"You never know what he's going to do," Gokok said.

"He has his reasons," the caretaker said.

"I came ten thousand miles just to go on this tour with him," the writer said.

"When you see him," Gokok said, "he'll tell you everything. Even of this conversation."

"You never know what he's going to do," the caretaker said.

"Isn't there some way I can catch up with him?" the writer asked.

The two men thought about this for a time, each suggesting possible solutions, but finally they decided it was not feasible. First of all, no one but Baba knew his itinerary and since he planned to tour many small villages and there would be no trains or buses to take the writer there, he would have to go by car. As Baba had already left four hours ago, it would be impossible to catch up with him now.

"Especially since we don't know where he's going," Gokok said.

Actually, the writer was not completely unhappy about missing the tour. The night before, about midnight, he began vomiting, having diarrhea at the same time, and shivering uncontrollably. He took his temperature and discovered with great alarm that it was a hundred and four.

Every few minutes he took the pills he had brought along for such emergencies, but each time vomited them up again immediately after swallowing them.

There was no possible way he could survive a two- or three-week tour through the villages, he decided. If eating the food which was prepared under sanitary conditions at Dr. Gokok's house could make him that sick, how could his body cope with the food in the villages? The first Indian newspaper he had seen when he got off the plane carried two small items so unnewsworthy they hardly rated mention. One told of forty-one people who had died after eating at the Calcutta airport canteen. The other reported seventy-eight students dead after eating at the cafeteria at Nehru Medical College. Twelve more were in critical condition.

What the hell was he doing in this stinkhole of a country chasing some nut who claimed to be God?

He put on all the clothes he had with him, including an overcoat, and crawled under all the blankets he could find. His teeth were chattering. The back of his head was throbbing with stupefying pain.

Finally, about four o'clock in the morning he dozed off. In a dream, or what seemed like a dream, he looked up and saw Baba standing at the foot of the bed. The writer was startled. He sat up. Baba just stood there, looking stern and quite clearly with disapproval, and then he disappeared.

The writer could hardly breathe. Nothing like this had ever happened to him before. He had no idea of whether he had just awakened or if he had been sleeping at all. He didn't know if what he saw was a dream or some kind of hallucination. Then he noticed, to his surprise, that he no longer was shivering. His nausea had gone and, taking his temperature, he noticed that so had his fever.

Earlier in the evening, before he got sick, he had been reading about Baba in the book Gokok had given him. A number of cases were reported in which Baba had appeared to his devotees in dreams, often to solve desperate problems for them and in some cases even to perform surgical operations. Baba was said to be able to leave his body and travel through astral time and space.

The cases made fascinating reading but none of them seemed credible, really, the writer decided. Having read the book caused him to have the dream and the fact that he no longer felt ill was nothing more than coincidental.

In the weeks to come as he waited for word from Baba, he spent his time interviewing as many people who knew Baba as he could and accumulated hundreds of stories, all extraordinary.

One man told of having cancer of the stomach. He had only a few weeks to live. One night Baba came to him in a dream, and, in the dream, operated on him. When the man awoke his bed was covered with blood, and there, beside him, was the cancer Baba had cut out.

"I cleaned it up myself," his wife said as the man proudly displayed the scar on his stomach.

A prominent dentist invited the writer to his home to see seven photographs of Baba, all with ashes pouring out of them.

"It started with this one," the dentist said, pointing to an eight-by-ten photograph of Baba. "Four days ago, right here on the glass, exactly where his hand is, as if coming out of the palm of his hand. And then we noticed the other pictures; in the big one, in the puja room, it started coming out of his mouth." The puja room was that part of every Hindu's house devoted exclusively for worship.

All of the photographs were bought in different places, the dentist said, and put in frames also bought in different places so there was no possibility of Baba or anyone else having treated them with some kind of chemical.

"Touch it, taste it, smell it," the dentist said. "Don't be afraid."

The writer took some of the *vibhuthi* (holy ashes) on his finger and smelled it. It smelled like incense.

"Taste it," the dentist said. "It's considered a great blessing."

The writer touched his finger to his tongue. It tasted sweet and pungent.

"I don't know why he picked us for such a great blessing," the dentist said.

A highly respected scientist told of a trip he had made with Baba to a beach at the southern tip of India.

"Baba stood on the seashore," he said, "and there were about one hundred, two hundred people. He had gone to stay with the governor of Kerala a couple of days and all these people gathered. So we all went to the seashore with him one day and when we got to the beach he stood on the sand and he said to the ocean, which was about thirty or forty feet away at the time, 'Well, you have called me here, what is it you want?' And the ocean, which had been very calm until he said that, suddenly started toward him, but only at that part of the beach where we were standing, and the water came right up to his feet, and stopped as if washing his feet, which is a common custom when a great man comes, when a religious head or something comes. It's an honor to wash his feet. So the sea came up and covered his feet completely and when the sea went back, around his feet there was a beautiful diamond necklace on the sand at his feet. Just once the sea came up, to leave the diamond necklace. A beautiful thing, costing, it must be, millions of rupees."

"You saw this with your own eyes?" the writer asked.

"Yes, yes, of course. With my own eyes. We all did."

A number of men who claimed to have been present told of an incident that they said occurred one day while Baba and a group of devotees were eating dinner at Puttaparthi. Baba's body suddenly grew stiff and for half an hour, they estimated, he didn't move. His pulse had stopped and so had all visible signs of breathing. Some of the devotees became alarmed, but many of those who had been with Baba for some time knew what was taking place and reassured those who were frightened that Baba had merely left his body.

When Baba finally regained consciousness he ordered a telegram to be sent immediately to a devotee in Bombay.

"Tell him don't worry, I have the revolver here," Baba said.

The telegram was sent but when Baba was asked where he had gone, what happened, he wouldn't tell them.

A few days later a letter arrived from the devotee in Bombay to whom Baba had sent the telegram. He was overcome with gratitude to Baba for having saved his life. The devotee had been unbearably despondent, he wrote, and was just about to shoot himself when somebody knocked at his door. Quickly he hid the gun under his pillow and opened the door to find two friends who had just dropped by for a chat. When they left, the devotee went to get the gun but it was gone. He looked everywhere for it and had no idea what could possibly have happened to it until he got Baba's telegram.

Often Baba left his body to be with a devotee at the moment of death. In almost every case a letter arrived a few days later, corroborating the death and the exact circumstances Baba had described.

On several occasions thousands of people witnessed Baba make it rain. On other occasions he had made it stop raining.

Once Baba materialized a gold medal that he was going to give to a violinist who had just finished a recital. Baba showed the medal to those around him but, remembering something, asked to have it back—explaining that he had forgotten the inscription. He held the medal in his hand for just a second and then gave it back to his devotees, who now saw engraved on the medal: "Presented by Bhagavan Sri Sathya Sai Baba to Vidway T. Chawdiah."

"See how quick my workmen are?" Baba said.

Once when Baba asked a devotee why he seemed so sad, the devotee told of having mistakenly spent a particular rupee that he wanted very much to save because a close friend of his who had now gone away had autographed it.

"Don't worry," Baba said, "it has now reached Bombay. I'll get it for you."

He closed his hand, seeming to take something from the air, and when he opened it the rupee with the autograph on it was in Baba's hand.

After two weeks the writer found himself unable to digest one more story about Baba's "miracles." Many were told to him by doctors, lawyers, scientists, educators, businessmen—all sound Establishment gentlemen who could not be mistaken for crackpots or religious fanatics. Others he

spoke with seemed less reliable. Many seemed to be repeating monologues they had perfected long ago. Others gave
the impression they were improvising the stories as they
went along.

Meanwhile, the writer fought his impatience. He knew
his time had not been wasted, but he resented having been
left behind. His anger had more to do with his own psycho-
logical problems than with the reality of the situation, and
recognizing this fact, he struggled to ignore his injured
pride and concentrate on the job he had come to do.

Having acquired more than enough testimony of Baba's
superhuman powers, the writer decided to go to Puttaparthi, where Baba was born.

The moment he saw the village the writer found himself
seized with panic. All of his life he had felt like an outsider
but now he felt outside of reality itself.

As the driver lifted the last suitcase from the top of the
taxi, the writer watched the dog who was having a fit howl
one last time, then whimper, then die.

❧ T W O

Originally, Puttaparthi was called Gollapalli, which means home of the cowherds. It was given this name not only in honor of Lord Krishna, the cowherd, but also because, according to the legend, the village was famous thousands of years ago as one of the most prosperous cattle-raising communities in the South. Everyone in the village owned cows which were healthy and beautiful and every home was rich with milk and butter. One day an anonymous cowherd noticed that his favorite cow had no milk in its udder when she came back from the grazing ground. There was also something mysterious about her behavior that led the cowherd to keep his eye on her. The next morning, a little before sunrise, the cow freed herself from the shed and, with the cowherd quietly following, crossed to the other side of the village, where she finally stopped beside a large ant hill. A moment later a cobra appeared from inside the ant hill; raising itself on its tail it began drinking from the cow's teat. Frightened, the cowherd picked up an enormous rock and threw it at the cobra. Before the snake died it put a curse on the village. Not only would all the cows in the community die, but in place of each cow a hundred ant hills would appear and begin to multiply endlessly, making the land untillable.

And so, of course, it came to pass and the name of the village was changed to Valmikipura (*valmika* means ant hill in Sanskrit). In time this name was reduced from the formal Sanskrit to the local vernacular. (*Putta* means ant hill and *parthi* means multiplier.)

As proof that this incident actually took place, a large stone, alleged to be the very stone which killed the snake, has been enshrined and a small temple built around it. The stone, about three feet high and a foot and a half wide, would seem to require at least two strong men just to lift it, but men were stronger in those days, a villager explained, and he pointed to the long reddish-brown line running the width of the stone.

"There is the blood of the cobra," he said, as if it would be impossible now to question its authenticity. Then suddenly, superstitiously, he kissed the stone and prostrated himself before it as if to ward off some specific misfortune which had occurred to him just that second.

Village Hinduism, as practiced by over eighty-five per cent of the people in India, has, on the surface, very little in common with the Hinduism most Westerners know from the Sanskrit classics. While most of the people in the villages have heard of Rama, Krishna, Vishnu and Siva, they generally worship one or a group of local deities, each family having a god or gods of its own. The complex variety of rituals are compulsively adhered to not for the elevation of the soul but simply as the only weapon they have to cope with the mysterious, hostile forces they feel have imprisoned them in this endless cycle of births and deaths.

The two most popular gods are Vishnu, the preserver, and Siva, who is believed to be both the creator and destroyer.

Vishnu, they believe, has reappeared in a number of incarnations. In one, as Krishna, the divine cowherd, he lived in the North where he performed numerous miracles and fell in love with a mortal, Radha, an affair which has inspired much of India's music, painting, and poetry.

Rama, another incarnation of Vishnu, is the subject of one of the two great Hindu epics, the Ramayana. It tells of the adventures of Rama in trying to save his wife, Sita, who had been kidnapped by a demon and carried off to Ceylon.

The other sacred Hindu epic is the Mahabharata. It contains one section, the Bagavadgita, that many scholars consider the core of Hinduism. This, too, is an adventure story of sorts about Arjuna, a warrior, who is forced by the circumstances of war to fight his own family and, Hamlet-like, goes through tortures of guilt and conscience wondering if rather than killing his own people he should not allow them to kill him instead. Finally he confides in his charioteer, who turns out to be the great God Krishna himself. Krishna explains that the death of loved ones is of no importance since all people are imperishable, and since Arjuna is a soldier, it is his duty, his *dharma*, to fight, with detachment, in the name of the Lord.

By Western standards Indian logic sometimes seems, at best, incomprehensible. The village of Puttaparthi, for example, is, as are most Indian villages, entirely agricultural and as such has quite correctly (according to Western logic) grown up near the banks of a river. But this river, about a hundred yards wide at the point it passes the village, is completely dry eight months a year; then the monsoons come, and for the other four months, year after year, it floods the countryside, washing away all but the sturdiest houses and most of the crops.

As for the narrow dusty paths (there are no roads), they seem not so much haphazard as absent-minded. Actually, only one pretzel-like trail services the village of Puttaparthi, having to curl around and around itself to accommodate the random arrangement of the houses. Occasionally an offshoot juts off tangentially into a plowed field as if either it had not been able to stop at the margin or else, in a spontaneous burst of self-expression, it had decided to go off on its own, only to have suddenly changed its mind about being a path at all.

The only vehicles of transportation are small, flat carts mounted on enormous wooden wheels, some almost six feet high. They are pulled by a pair of scrawny, unmanageable bullocks. The women also function, in part, as beasts of burden. They are responsible for carrying, on their heads, large earthenware jugs full of water from the community well, half a mile from the village. They also carry, again on their heads, the dried mud bricks and mortar used in the construction of houses.

The houses usually consist of one windowless room about six feet long and four or five feet wide, with mud floors coated with a thin paste made of cow dung and water.

Cooking is done in a pot supported by two small ridges of dried mud over a fire of dried cow-dung cakes. Cow dung is so valuable that it is constantly sought after, even fought over, by women and boys who race for the droppings the moment they plop to the ground. It is of great importance for the villagers to pile up enough dried cakes during the drought to last them through the floods.

Many homes are beginning to have one-burner kerosene stoves for cooking but these produce so much smoke and such an unpleasant odor that most of the wives prefer cow dung.

The more affluent homes may reserve one corner of the courtyard for taking baths—water splashed from jugs. No toilets exist. The nearest field is considered the proper place to relieve oneself, but even this function is subject to a rigid set of rules, making it more a religious experience than a simple act of nature.

It is perfectly all right to empty the bowels or the bladder in sight of a person from a lower caste but one must never do this in the presence of a Brahmin or a cow. One must squat as low as possible (men even squat to urinate) and while in this position one must not, under any circumstance, even inadvertently, look at the sun, the moon, the stars, fire, a temple, or an idol. Complete silence is demanded and speed desired. When the act has been completed, the part of the body employed must be washed but only the left hand may be used to wash it. The water is in a cup one has brought along for the purpose. In these confusing times the cup usually is of plastic or else an empty tin can is used. It is absolutely forbidden to use the right hand, even to carry the cup to the fields. The right hand is for eating and worship and must be kept pure and holy, just as the left hand is considered contaminated and may never be used to touch food or religious objects.

The actual ritual of elimination depends upon the specific compulsions of the individual. Many insist upon washing each part of the body below the waist five times, always starting with the right foot. The exact order of when each of the other parts are washed varies according to caste, family custom, or individual superstition.

These rules, incidentally, apply not only to people in the villages but in varying degrees to all but the most sophisticated Hindus. Every bus and train traveling through the countryside stops periodically to allow the passengers to scatter in the fields, and in the cities where no fields are available it is not uncommon to see adults and children of both sexes defecating on the sidewalks.

Over four hundred million people, according to a recent estimate, live and die in the villages of India and almost none of them has ever seen an automobile or electricity. Some may have heard of telephones, refrigerators, washing machines, television sets, but these conveniences—taken for granted by all but the most deprived people in most of the countries of the world—have less reality to the people in the villages of India than naked Siva, the destroyer, with his blue throat and his red skin and the garland of snakes in his hair or Nandi, the bull without blemish, he rides on.

In Puttaparthi, however, which in most aspects differs hardly at all from almost any other village in the South, the people are unique in one important way. The twentieth century has come to their door. Prosperity has returned, not in the form of cattle but in the form of Sathya Sai Baba. Out of an estimated following of more than six million people, nearly a million pilgrims from many countries of the world come to Puttaparthi every year. Most of them come fully expecting Baba to perform a miracle.

The majority of pilgrims who come have physical afflictions to be cured but every conceivable kind of problem has been brought to Baba since 1940, when his powers were revealed. If one can form a judgment from the growth of his fame year by year, it would seem that a convincingly large number of those who come to him find a measure of satisfaction in some way. In a land where holy men, yogis, and magicians can be found in overabundance a short spit away from almost anywhere, only Sai Baba is considered by all factions, even his detractors, to be a major force in the country.

Baba's ashram at Puttaparthi is not technically in Puttaparthi at all. It is a complete compound within itself, begun in 1950 and in 1966 declared by the government of India to be a legal township called Prasanthi Nilayam (the home of highest peace). The main gate is only a few hundred feet from the village and along the bumpy dirt path, which leads from the village to the ashram and curves around it, an assortment of crude stalls have been set up more to take advantage of the stream of pilgrims than to accommodate them. Two laundries compete for the business of those visitors rich enough not to have to wash their own saris and dhotis. Five bathhouses (for men only) offer to those who can afford it an earthenware jug of tepid water and two square feet of space vaguely partitioned by narrow straw mats hung down to the waist from the ceiling. No soap. No towels.

Two mud huts, one called a coffee house and the other The Brahman Hotel, sell cooked food. There is a stall that sells raw grain, fruits, and vegetables, and another that sells fly-covered sweets and a kind of drink only remotely suggesting the flavor of an orange. There are more than a dozen stalls, most of them devoted exclusively to selling souvenirs of Sai Baba. Photographs ranging from huge tinted posters to tiny black and white snapshots are available for a price, either framed or unframed. Rings with Baba's picture on them, incense holders with his picture on them, even campaign buttons with his picture on them are available, and the prices vary from hour to hour, from person to person, depending entirely upon the merchant's spontaneous opinion of how much the customer might be willing to pay. Unlike conventional bazaars, however, no bargaining takes place. Even though the merchant may quote a number of different prices to the same person for the same item at different times, once he has said the price there is no possibility for negotiation even if he is reminded that he offered the same piece of merchandise for a lower price or a higher one minutes before. He doesn't dispute the fact. He simply doesn't hear it.

Dozens of women gather at the gates of the ashram each day, many having walked for miles with baskets of emaciated fruit, nuts, or vegetables on their heads, and they sit on the ground all day, if necessary, until they have sold the last of their bananas, most no bigger than four inches long, or the very last peanut, each the size of a green pea.

And the beggars, of course, always the beggars, including those women who shove grotesquely deformed children in front of foreigners especially, knowing that even the most hard-hearted Westerner can never refuse a crippled child.

It is said that to aid in begging, these women deliberately cut off the arms and legs of their children at birth or keep their limbs bound and twisted until they grow into indescribable parodies of the human form. It is easy to believe these stories—having seen the women.

For the people of Puttaparthi, Sai Baba has become a flourishing industry and, while there are no signs of wealth visible to a middle-class American, ask any person in the village and he will tell you with undisguised envy that his neighbor is growing rich.

❧ THREE

At twelve minutes after four the four o'clock bell was rung in the prayer hall. (A few minutes one way or the other means very little to people absorbed with Eternity.)

Since most of the people in the ashram have no clock or watch, the purpose of the bell is to let the pilgrims know each morning when it is time to get up. At least half of them on this particular morning were already awake and hundreds of men, women, and children could be seen as vague shadows in the dark making their way in all directions from the compound to the surrounding fields, a plastic cup or tin can in each left hand.

By noon the temperature would climb to a hundred and ten in the shade but at this hour there was a sharp chill in the air. The two rows of coconut trees, one on each side of the dirt road leading from the main gate to the prayer hall, should have seemed romantic, backlighted as they were by an almost full moon but in the context of the immediate surroundings it only added an additional touch of the surreal to an already eerie landscape.

A shed, a hundred feet long and forty feet wide with a tin roof and a stone floor but no walls, stood between the main gate and the prayer hall. It was built to house the transient pilgrims, who may number anywhere from a thousand on ordinary days to a hundred thousand on the holiest day. On this particular morning, nineteen days before one of the festivals, about two thousand people, including many families with small children, already had filled the shed. The overflow had nearly filled the adjacent uncompleted shed, which also had a tin roof but no floor.

The festival was called Shivarathri, "The Night of Siva." It celebrates the marriage of Siva to Parvati. For twenty-four hours the devotees are expected to fast, and (at Baba's ashram) they sit on the ground singing *bhajans* (holy songs) all night. They sit in front of the temple facing a pink and yellow stucco structure, which looks like an Indian version of a bandstand in a small New England town. At the climax of the ceremony Baba appears on the platform, which is only used once a year, on Shivarathri. He begins to speak but every year since he revealed himself to be holy, he has been interrupted by painful convulsions in his stomach. After several minutes of what some observers have described as "labor pains," a number of lingams are ejected from his mouth. A lingam is the phallic symbol used in the worship of Siva to represent his generative powers. Frequently, according to those who have witnessed the event, a lingam has been so large the corners of Baba's mouth were ripped as it came out. They are most often made of gold or silver. After letting the crowd see the figures, Baba gives them to various devotees to keep. Many of his followers consider receiving a *Shivalingam* from Baba the highest honor Baba can bestow on them short of granting them an end to the cycle of births and deaths.

"At least a hundred thousand people will be here this

year," one of the permanent residents had predicted to the writer his first evening at the ashram, and the five or six other men, all in their sixties and seventies, who were standing around, made that peculiar motion of their heads which means "no" in America but "yes" in South India.

Except for the few others who might be able to squeeze into the uncompleted shed, the rest of the pilgrims who would arrive in the days to come would have to sleep in the fields. As uncomfortable as this might seem to a comfort-oriented Westerner, living conditions for most of the people in the sheds were not all that different from what they had at home. They slept on the floor at home exactly as they were doing here with almost as little privacy, and having literally no possessions except the few absolute essentials which even at home they keep padlocked in a small tin chest, they were able with very little difficulty to bring everything they owned with them.

The possessions for an average family consist of a copper pot or two for cooking, a couple of earthenware jugs for carrying and storing water, a cotton quilt or two, enough cups for the left hand, and one stainless steel cup for drinking which is used by the whole family, none of whom may allow the cup to touch their lips. Many families in the sheds had kerosene stoves to cook on and the men who shaved had double-edged safety razors and small stainless-steel mirrors. Some members of the upper-middle class had a small jar of instant coffee and the really affluent had a small package of powdered milk.

Each person or family unit had set up housekeeping of sorts in the few feet of space they had appropriated, the elaborateness dictated by personality and the degree of affluence. Almost every unit had a picture of Baba prominently displayed on an improvised altar where puja, the ritual of prayer, was performed; and while Baba occupied the most honored position, he was flanked in many cases by pictures of the family god or gods.

By twenty minutes after four all of the people in both sheds were awake and busily involved in the start of a new day.

There was no talking, none. And strangely, in the darkness, there seemed to be no need for talking. There was only purposeful movement in the shadows, in the heavy yet strangely agile silence. From the far end of the main shed came the sound of a baby crying. A chronic asthmatic could be heard desperately wheezing in the other shed. Then from still another direction came the tortured clearing of a congested throat, then another, then another. Gradually, from all directions, a chorus of coughing began, building and blending contrapuntally into a tubercular fugue.

A blind man, about sixty, with a bald head, ragged beard, and fierce pride, was being led from the shed toward the main gate by a shaven-headed boy, about eight. From the other direction came a man in his late thirties who carried, on his back, a teen-age boy with polio. The man smiled warmly at the boy leading the blind man, but the boy just looked at him without smiling, but also without hostility.

When the man with the boy on his back got to the prayer hall he stopped and reached around to lift the boy off his back, but in doing so he lost his balance. Both he and the boy fell, the boy's legs sprawling grotesquely in the dirt. Quickly, the boy looked up and caught the eyes of a stranger, who looked away. For a moment the boy watched the stranger not look at him, embarrassed to have fallen but even more embarrassed to have been caught looking to see if anyone had seen him. The father looked at the stranger, too, and with no self-consciousness laughed. Then he lifted the boy to a sitting position facing the prayer hall. He too turned toward the prayer hall and stretched out full length, face down, to pay homage to Baba by prostrating himself in the dirt. There was a joy in this man which separated him from the others, many of whom radiated bliss, tranquillity, even ecstasy but no one else had his uncomplicated, never-wavering delight in the simple pleasure of being alive.

Nearby a tall fat man, walking quickly like a person from a city, blew his nose into the fingers of his left hand, flinging the mucus to the ground without bothering to notice a small white sign nailed to the palm tree he was passing at the time: "Don't Spit Here."

A young woman with half her face eaten away by what seemed to be leprosy was walking around and around the temple with a sense of purpose which indicated that a specific number of circumlocutions were required. All the while she kept repeating the same muttered prayer to herself. At one point she barely avoided colliding with another woman, in her seventies, coming from the opposite direction but also going around and around the temple, stopping only to kiss each wall and quietly breathe a prayer.

A girl about six was leading a blind girl about nine toward the main shed.

A small man, about fifty, with a beatific glow, was slowly turning around and around in front of a small lingam which was part of a circular fence around what looked as if it might once have been a flower garden. As the man turned, his eyes were closed as if in a dream, and his lips, over and over, silently mouthed a prayer.

On the other side of the temple a tall young Brahmin with a British officer's mustache and one leg shorter than the other was unlocking the leg of an elephant chained to a palm tree.

"*Namaske*," he said to the elephant when the animal was free. He bowed respectfully, the palms of both hands together in front of his face.

The elephant bent his right front leg and bowed, returning the salute, and then he followed the young man three times around the prayer hall, stopping each time at the front of the building to bow to the idea of Baba.

At the side of the road a woman in her sixties was doubled over, vomiting.

Near the village road several women were clanging the heavy chains as they pulled up water at the ashram well.

On the village road the beggars already had taken their places just outside the ashram gate. The blind man was led outside the gate by the little boy, who waited with irritable impatience as the blind man lit a cigarette, savoring the first puff. Since no smoking was permitted inside the ashram, this one smoke would have to last the old man most of the day.

None of the stalls was open yet but eight or nine men were warming themselves in front of one of the laundries, silently standing around the fire as a girl, about seven, put pieces of red-hot coals into a large hand iron which she then closed and, using a piece of cloth spread on the dirt as an ironing board, started pressing the pile of laundry in the basket beside her. A mongrel with every rib showing under its tightly stretched, sore-covered skin walked aimlessly by, growling to itself as most of the starving dogs in India do.

Suddenly, with no apparent provocation, one of the men by the fire picked up a stone and threw it as hard as he could, hitting the dog on the side. The dog yelped but didn't run, apparently too lethargic from malnutrition to care. The man yelled something at the dog in one of the Indian languages as he bent to pick up another rock, but the dog started casually walking away and the man apparently didn't feel the need to throw the second stone. Instead, he held it a moment in his hand as if suddenly struck with the profound revelation that it was in some way extraordinary for a man to hold a stone in his hand. Then, for reasons known only to himself, he kissed the rock as if it were holy and showed it to the other men.

"Sai Ram," he said to no one in particular, taking the name of Sai Baba and linking it with Rama, one of the incarnations of God.

"Sai Ram," the others said.

Sai Ram.

Portrait of Shirdi Sai Baba, painted from one of the few existing photographs of him.

Baba as a young man during *bhajan* classes.

Baba speaking to his followers. *John Worldlie*

Men waiting for Baba in front of prayer hall. Women's section in background, extreme right.

Baba officiating at a special ceremony outside his temple at Prasanthi Nilayam. *John Worldlie*

Baba speaking to a group of devotees from the balcony of the temple at Prasanthi Nilayam. *John Worldlie*

❦ FOUR

Her name is Asha for the purpose of this account, although
why she was so adamant about her real name not being used
was unclear even to her.

"Perhaps," she suggested, "spending one's life in politics
makes one uncommonly cautious." Then she laughed and
changed the word to suspicious.

She was twenty-seven, a few inches taller than average,
with definite yet delicate features made all the more striking
by the majestic mien she adopted with no trace of pretension
or self-consciousness.

She lived in an expensive apartment, newly built, in a section of New Delhi chiefly populated by well-connected
young couples.

As she later recalled, trying to reconstruct the order of
events, she awoke about four o'clock in the morning on the
day she made the decision. She looked at the clock beside
her bed to see how much more of the night was left to be
endured. She had recently become addicted to sleeping pills
and as she lay in the dark struggling to prevent another anxiety attack, she decided to try to make it until breakfast

without taking either barbiturates or a tranquilizer. The dosage needed to put her to sleep had increased so rapidly the most she could hope for now was an hour or two of sleep in exchange for three Seconals.

She was the only daughter of a diplomat whose foreign assignments had begun when she was eleven. He took her to various capital cities in Europe, where she grew up neither Indian nor European. Periodically she'd return to India when her father got home leave but the rarefied atmosphere in which they lived went with them, encasing her in an airtight bubble of exclusivity.

When her father suggested that Asha meet a young man who, he thought, might make her a good husband, he made it seem enough like the usual arranged marriage to appeal to the sense of tradition he had so carefully instilled in her, but with just enough humor so that her sense of being a thoroughly liberated twentieth-century female was not in any way offended.

The young man was five years older than she, not at all bad looking, from a highly compatible family, had a promising future, and, her father added, knowing she would take it as a joke, their horoscopes matched.

She laughed, but she knew that both families had, indeed, consulted the same astrologer her grandparents had gone to before arranging the marriage of her parents.

The concept of marriage in India is more a question of two harmonious families merging than the accident of two people finding each other sexually attractive, so at the first meeting of an arranged marriage all of the members of both families are present. In this case both families were sophisticated enough to make light of the occasion, thereby putting enormous pressure on the couple by the simple expedient of seeming to put no pressure on them at all.

She had always planned to marry an Indian, never letting

herself get really serious about any of the young men she dated abroad (although once at college in England she forced herself to stop seeing the son of a Brazilian ambassador when she realized they could have, and maybe even had, fallen in love with each other).

Even though she had never really lived as an Indian, she felt Indian, more out of a sentimental need for a culture to belong to than out of the understanding of the realities of what spending her life as an Indian woman would mean.

The first meeting went well enough for the young man to call her several days later and ask for a date, a concession both families were willing to tolerate in deference to the modern world. Strictly according to custom, the couple should never be permitted together unless accompanied by a married relative.

They both laughed about the absurdity of arranged marriages in these times, but they both wanted such a marriage enough to allow themselves to fall in love after only five dates.

She was married at twenty-three, and she and her husband moved into the two-bedroom apartment where she now lived, on the ground floor of a complex of two-story houses, each with a little lawn and flower bed.

She had a Brahmin cook, since only Brahmins are allowed to touch the food of other Brahmins, an ayah to take care of their son, born thirteen months after they were married, and a sweeper who did the heavy housework. The cook and the sweeper lived in the servants' quarters behind the apartment complex, but the ayah lived in the apartment, sleeping on the floor in the child's room.

The kitchen was equipped with a rented two-burner gas stove like the ones in the apartments of all of her friends, but only she had an imported refrigerator. The Indian government has made it almost impossible for an Indian to import

anything, but she was determined to have at least the basic
conveniences she had grown up with. Utilizing all of her
father's connections, she gradually accumulated what her
friends considered an astonishing number of Western appli-
ances. Even her saris, mostly made of nylon, were imported.
She had a Japanese record player, an Italian typewriter, a
hair dryer and a toaster from America, and a German automobile.

She spoke Hindi, fluent English, passable French and Punjabi, which was the language spoken in the region where her
father was born.

Her husband spoke Punjabi, Hindi, and English, but because he spoke Spanish instead of French, his first post in the
foreign service was in Argentina. After three years he had
been transferred back to New Delhi, and now after two
years he had been scheduled for a posting somewhere in the
Middle East when suddenly it was discovered he had cancer
of the ears and throat—already so advanced it was considered inoperable.

Her father took his son-in-law's x-rays to Bombay for the
most famous specialist in India to examine, but it was no use,
he was told. All they could pray for was a quick death instead of a long and lingering one.

He had been in the hospital for two months. For the past
two weeks he had been neither able to speak nor to hear and
since the pain was unbearable, he was kept under heavy
sedation at all times.

Her life before the illness now seemed so shallow she
wondered how she had managed to bear it.

Every morning began exactly the same way. At eight
o'clock the alarm clock rang. She would roll over and put
the pillow over her head. Her husband would get out of bed
immediately. He allowed her to squeeze out the last few

drops of sleep and then he would call to her gently, from the bathroom. Finally she would sit up in bed and shout to their ayah, Lakshmi, in the kitchen.

"*Chai lao!*" (bring the tea now).

Asha hated Lakshmi, especially in the morning. All of her friends hated their servants and much of their conversation concerned how hopelessly incompetent, lazy, and dishonest they were.

While Asha's husband shaved in the bathroom, she remained in bed waiting for Lakshmi to bring the tea. Every three or four minutes Asha would yell all kinds of threats toward the kitchen, demanding that the tea be brought immediately.

When Lakshmi would call back that it was coming, she was on her way, that meant it was only about ten minutes before she'd be ready. Until then the ayah didn't bother to answer.

"If you got up when you're supposed to," Asha would yell, "you'd have the tea ready when you're supposed to."

The tea was supposed to be ready the instant Asha called for it, but Lakshmi never awoke until she heard Asha yelling and every morning Asha and her husband had to wait until Lakshmi pulled herself together, went to the kitchen, dropped a few utensils, broke a few pieces of china, then put the water on to boil.

As they waited Asha and her husband would shout back and forth to each other from room to room discussing social plans and household problems.

The bathroom contained a Western-style toilet that only occasionally flushed. There was no bathtub or sink, only a shower head on a pipe sticking out of the wall about five feet from the floor. The water was permitted to splash all over the room, draining out through a hole in the far corner.

There was no hot water, so in the winter Lakshmi was

supposed to turn on the electric water heater in the kitchen a half hour before Asha and her husband awoke and have a pail of hot water ready for the master's bath, but since Lakshmi never woke up until she was called, he was never permitted the luxury of bathing with hot water. He had to get to work and couldn't wait.

Finally, in her own good time, Lakshmi would appear with tea, sugar, and milk on a tray. Both Asha and her husband were watching their weight so they had given up the bed-tea biscuits customarily served at this time. As he dressed he sipped tea with Asha in the bedroom. He wore Western-style shoes and pants, and the traditional Indian dress coat, which during its brief period of popularity in the West was known as a Nehru jacket. When he was ready for work she put on her dressing gown and they went out for breakfast to the section of the living room which served as a dining area. The Brahmin cook served them two boiled eggs each, with marmalade, toast, and, again, tea with milk.

After breakfast her husband went to the office and Asha would bathe. Both winter and summer Asha preferred the Indian version of a bath to the shower. As all of her friends did, she would sit on the standard small stool near a second faucet which stuck out of the wall several feet below the shower. In winter she would dilute the half-bucket of hot water Lakshmi brought her with cold water from the tap, then she would splash it on to herself with a pink plastic cup, first to wet her body, then, after soaping herself, to rinse the lather on to the floor.

It took her a long time to dress and get made-up. She was by nature a dawdler and in the morning when she was alone she gave in to this indulgence. Then she gave the cook the menus for dinner and lunch, and every third day she would go to the food market to shop for meat, fish, chicken, and various household items that she didn't trust the cook to buy, not so much because he considered it part of his job to steal a certain percentage of the money she gave him, but more importantly, he couldn't be relied upon to bother to take the time to search properly for the best quality.

The ayah bathed the child and cared for him while Asha prepared for the routine diplomatic cocktail parties, embassy dinners, and women's organization teas she was expected to attend.

All morning the telephone in Asha's apartment was in constant use as she coordinated plans and exchanged gossip with her friends, being constantly interrupted during the early hours by the cook, who came to tell her the bread wallah was here, the milk wallah was here, the vegetable wallah was here. In the old days when Asha was a child, it was not considered proper for mem-sahib to concern herself with what took place in the kitchen. Her sense of social consciousness branded such aristocracy decadent, but when her conscience wasn't looking, she secretly longed to return to those days.

After the phone calls and marketing had been taken care of, she frequently washed and set her own hair. About once a month, for important official occasions, she went to a beauty parlor.

Afternoons were spent either at cocktail parties or women's club meetings where in most cases a very minor dignitary would give an insufferably boring lecture about religion, philosophy, or the arts, after which coffee would be served and more gossip exchanged.

At six-thirty her husband would return from work. They had tea again, with fried snacks this time. *Pakoras* (vegetables fried in batter) were his favorite. After tea her husband would read the newspaper or play with the child while she supervised dinner. About eight-thirty they would eat their main meal. This always consisted of chapatis, a meat curry, and a vegetable served Western style on plates instead of on palm leaves and eaten with knives and forks instead of, as most Indians did, with their fingers.

On the morning she made her decision she lay in bed watching the darkness drain from the night. The temptation to get up and take three more Seconals had become almost irresistible when suddenly she thought: "Oh my God! I forgot to take the pill last night." Then, with a start, she remembered she had stopped taking the birth control pills two months ago when her husband went into the hospital.

She got out of bed and took two tranquilizers. Her husband was almost dead. That was the reality. A widow in India is expected to remain one until she dies, but she was a modern woman first, she realized, an Indian second. In time she would consider the idea of getting married again, she knew that, and that was a reality she could not begin to cope with at the moment.

Since her husband had been in the hospital she was not expected to participate in any of the social activities her life previously had been entirely concerned with, and now that she had no function she felt she had no identity. Neither she nor anything that was happening was real, she decided, even though she knew that it was her life until now that had been unreal. This was Reality, this panic in a dark room. She was drowning in Reality, without even the protection of an identity.

Most of her time in the past two months had been spent waiting at the hospital, either watching her husband lie there like a vegetable or, when she could no longer stand it, waiting outside in the reception room with friends or members of the family.

Usually the visitors stayed only a short time, for which she was grateful, because there was nothing to say and nothing to do, and the pressure of trying to force herself to maintain one end of a conversation going nowhere was exhausting. It didn't seem proper to gossip, but without being able to gossip neither she nor her friends had anything to talk about.

Her father's sister had come to the hospital the day before and after taking one look at Asha insisted they go to the Oberoi Intercontinental Hotel for lunch.

Neither Asha nor any of her friends could afford lunch at the Intercontinental, and ordinarily it would have been considered a great treat; but under the circumstances Asha found it an effort to make conversation and so did her aunt. For long periods of time they sat quietly at one of the tables on the lawn behind the hotel watching the black birds walk from plate to plate on their table, finishing the lunch which neither of them had more than politely touched.

Just before they left, while they were waiting for the waiter to bring the check, her aunt casually mentioned a holy man somewhere in South India who, she had heard, performed miraculous cures. A friend of the aunt's was a friend of a friend of the scientific adviser to the minister of defense, who, the aunt had heard, had a son who was born crippled and all of the doctors the boy was taken to said his condition was hopeless. For some reason (the aunt was not clear why) the scientist took the boy to see this holy man, who, without having been told anything, gave a precise diagnosis in exact medical terms of what was wrong with the boy and offered to perform an operation on the boy's spine right there on the floor of the room where they were sitting. For some reason, which the scientist even at the time could not understand, he agreed to let the holy man perform the operation, even though he had very little formal education and no medical training whatsoever. The holy man waved his hand in the air, the aunt had been told, and materialized

all of the complicated instruments necessary for the operation. Then he materialized some *vibhuthi* which he rubbed
on the boy's back, saying this would prevent the boy from
feeling any pain. As he performed the operation he got
blood all over his own hands, the aunt had heard, but none
on the boy's body.

When the holy man finished, he asked one of the devotees
who had watched the operation for a towel. For a time all of
the devotees searched everywhere in the house but could
not find one.

"If you materialized all of those other things," the boy's
father said, "why can't you materialize a towel?"

The holy man laughed. He hadn't thought of that. With
another wave of his hand he materialized a towel.

"The boy is able to walk now," the aunt said. "Perfectly."
And then she added: "You can meet him if you want to.
And his father, too, if you want to."

At the time Asha was annoyed. Her aunt, who was married to an important industrialist, was not ordinarily given
to this sort of holy man rubbish, and she resented having
been told the story.

"Not right now," Asha said.

"It wouldn't hurt to explore it," the aunt said.

"Please!" Asha said. "I don't want to discuss it."

Asha went to her medicine chest and took two tranquilizers before she remembered she had just taken two, then
she sat on the edge of the bed, astonished to find herself
seriously considering this holy man. Although she knew
the idea was totally absurd, she decided to call her aunt and
find out the name of the saint or whatever he was, and possibly fly down to see him. The only thing that worried her
was what she would tell her friends.

✿ FIVE

By four-thirty in the morning the prayer hall at the ashram in Puttaparthi was completely filled, the women on the left side of the high-ceilinged room, the men on the right side. The hall is about thirty feet long, twenty feet wide, with photographs and drawings of Hindu gods and Christian saints hung side by side along three walls. Along the fourth wall, at the front of the room, is a small stage with a larger than life size, hand-tinted photograph of Baba on one side of the silver throne where Baba sits on special occasions. On the other side there is a similar photograph of a thin, sad-faced old man with a short white beard whom Baba refers to as "my previous body," claiming to be a reincarnation of the old man, a cantankerous saint who died in 1918, eight years before the present Sai Baba was born. To distinguish between the two the old man is known as Shirdi Sai Baba, Shirdi being the name of an otherwise undistinguished village about one hundred fifty miles north of Bombay where the old man lived. Baba from Puttaparthi is known as Sathya Sai Baba, Sathya being a diminutive for Sathyanarayana, the name he was given at birth. Actually Sai Baba is not a name at all. *Sai* is a Persian word for saint and *Baba* a Hindi term of endearment and respect meaning, roughly, little father.

Since 1940, when Sathya first announced that he was Sai Baba reincarnated, a number of the old man's devotees have made the pilgrimage to Puttaparthi to challenge the young man. There is no record of the number of people who went away unimpressed but dozens of doubters have documented how they were convinced.

One of the more notable converts was the Rani of Chinchali whose husband, the raja, was a devotee of Shirdi Sai Baba. Some time after her husband's death the rani heard about this boy from Puttaparthi (he was fifteen at the time) who claimed to be the incarnation of her husband's master, so she went to Puttaparthi to question the boy.

Time after time, she recalled, Baba astonished her with answers to questions only Shirdi could have known. But as she still had lingering doubts, she asked Baba to go with her to her home at Chinchali, then to her palace at Hyderabad where he continued to amaze her with his knowledge of her life with the raja and their experiences with Shirdi. At one point Baba described in exact detail the changes which had been made in the palace and the grounds since he had seen them in his previous body. On another occasion he asked her about a small stone image of Anjaneya which had been given to the raja by Shirdi. She didn't remember the statue until Baba told her exactly where it was, in an out-of-the-way corner of the palace, and then he told her in detail of the circumstances in which the raja came to receive it. He finally erased all doubts, she remembered, when he described a photograph of Shirdi the raja once had taken. The rani could not remember the photograph until Baba again told her exactly where in the palace she could find it. Then he refreshed her memory of the day the picture had been taken, recalling the precise circumstances of how and when and why and where Shirdi had agreed to pose, including many details only she and the raja and Shirdi could have known.

One woman in her sixties, now a permanent resident at Baba's ashram, tells how she was convinced Sathya Sai is the incarnation of Shirdi Sai. In 1917, she remembers, she went to the old man at Shirdi after the sudden death of her four children. Life had no meaning for her any longer and, hearing of the saint, she made the trip to see him as a last, desperate measure. As soon as she saw the old man she knew in one profound moment of enlightenment that she had found the peace and spirituality she had been looking for, and she begged him to let her stay with him the rest of her life.

"Not now," he told her. "I will come again in another body in the South. Then you will stay with me there."

Reluctantly obeying her master, she returned to her village and established a home for orphan girls in his name and thought no more about what he had said until years later, when she heard about the boy in the South who claimed to be Sai Baba. She went immediately to see him, and when she got there, she reports, Baba spoke to her softly in Hindi as Shirdi used to do instead of in Telugu, the native language of Sathya Sai.

"So you have come, my child," he said to her. "Give me the sixteen rupees you owe me."

"What sixteen rupees?" she asked.

"Out of the money you saved to be sent to me at Shirdi for the Dasara celebrations. Don't you remember? You lent Balaram forty rupees, but he only returned twenty-four."

Suddenly she remembered the incident he mentioned.

"I am asking you this only to convince you I am Shirdi," he said.

She began to cry.

"Stop crying," he said. "I told you I would see you again

and where I would see you again, yet you come with so little faith you sit down as soon as you come in. Get up and do what you used to do. Don't you touch my feet any more?"

The *sais* come in a series, Sathya Sai has said, and when he has left his present body another *sai*, Prema Sai Baba, will be born in the adjoining State of Mysore.

At four-fifty the morning session began in the prayer hall, as usual, with the rapid ringing of a large bell hung from the ceiling at the back of the room. Its deafening sound was apparently designed to shatter the illusionary world in preparation for entering that of the Absolute. With the sound of the bell still silently vibrating in the room, the group began to chant "Om" twenty-one times, each sound held half a minute or more until each long breath had slowly and rhythmically expired. Then a woman in the front row began playing a harmonium, an instrument first brought to India by the Christian missionaries, and the group began singing *bhajans*. These religious songs usually are in worship of Baba, praising his wondrous ways, but often they also offer prayers to Siva, or Krishna. Half an hour later the singing ends with a song that keeps accelerating in tempo. The worshipers clap their hands to the quickening beat and, finally, when they are clapping and singing as fast as they can, everybody cheers, "*Jai Sai Baba! Jai! Jai!*" This either means "Victory to Sai" or "Glory to Sai," depending on who is translating. At this point a priest walks through the hall with lighted camphor on a silver tray. Frantically, the members of the congregation stand on tiptoes, maneuvering around each other, pushing, shoving to make beckoning motions toward the camphor as if trying to entice the magical powers of its aroma from the tray to their eyes and head.

Most of the women and many of the men leave after this ceremony, but about one-third generally stay for half an hour of meditation.

On this particular morning Mr. Desai, the man with the teen-age son who had polio, went through the camphor ritual with joy and passion, as he always did, and his son went through the motions as he always did, mechanically and without conviction.

Occasionally they stayed for the meditation but on this particular morning Mr. Desai was hungry. He was so hungry, in fact, that he decided not to cook breakfast for himself and his son as he usually did, but to go to the ashram canteen instead. He picked up his son and carried him as he always did, on his back, through the scattered group of men who had already begun their meditation. At one point he stopped to openly admire a young monk sitting in the full lotus position. He wore a saffron robe, his shoulder-length hair matted with cow dung as a form of worship. This was the kind of total dedication Desai wished circumstances had permitted him to pursue. Perhaps in another life, he consoled himself, he would be elevated from the ranks of a householder to that of the sadhu.

The next prayer session was not until seven-thirty, and the time until then was supposed to be used first for bathing and then for breakfast, but Mr. Desai was so hungry he decided to eat first and bathe after.

Baba still had not returned to the ashram. For nearly three weeks he had been touring Andhra Pradesh, and for the people waiting to see him the principal diversion was exchanging rumors about where Baba might now be and when he might be expected to return. That is, for those few who could speak the same language. There are no exact figures readily available as to the actual number of languages and dialects spoken in India, but according to one set of figures there are 179 different languages and 533 different dialects, all of which makes it almost impossible for one uneducated Indian to communicate with another unless he happens to come from the same region. Consequently, newcomers to the ashram quickly found their own group, creating a number of isolated ghettos, clung to as much for moral support as for companionship.

Mr. Desai walked through the crowd outside the prayer hall like a man at a carnival, greeting those he had already become acquainted with and smiling at everyone who caught his eye.

On the way to the canteen he stopped briefly to exchange greetings with Mr. Rao, a tailor from a village near Mangalore, on the Southern coast. Rao was an unusually tall man for an Indian, skeleton-thin, with a long neck and a caricature of an Adam's apple. He was wearing a plain brown Western-style short-sleeved sport shirt which hung over his dhoti.

"Sai Ram," Rao said.

"Sai Ram," Desai said.

Neither the words "hello," "good-by," nor the usual Indian greeting of *Namaske* are used at the ashram in deference to the idea that God's name should always be on one's tongue and mind.

"Did you hear about Kasturi?" Rao asked. Kasturi, in his seventies, has served Baba exclusively since 1948 when Baba designated him his official biographer. Since then Kasturi has recorded and translated all of Baba's major speeches in addition to writing a two-volume biography, which has been printed at the ashram on a fifty-year-old hand press. (One of these was the book Gokok had given the writer.) As a member of the innermost circle Kasturi has more prestige than anyone else in the ashram with the possible exception of Raj Reddy, the son of a maharaja, who is Baba's personal chauffeur and all around right-hand man.

The rumor that Kasturi had received a letter from Baba had been circulating since yesterday, and according to the rumor (neither Desai nor Rao had bothered to check it with Kasturi), Baba had written from Madras to say that after a day or two there he would proceed to Bangalore.

"Yes, I heard," Desai said.

"If he spends two or three days in Madras," Rao said, "he will not get to Bangalore until Monday, and then I understand he's beginning a college there in Bangalore, so that will take some time. So we can figure he won't be here until at least a week unless he spends more time in Madras, but then he might not go to Bangalore because he'll have to prepare himself here for Shivarathri. But I was talking to a man from Madras who knows the man Baba is staying with and he said this man is forming a Sathya Sai organization in Madras, so if that is the case, perhaps he will have to stay longer, but then again, perhaps not."

Rao had come to Puttaparthi the year before but had to leave before he got a private interview with Baba because his sister wrote him she was not well. Since then he had gone deeper and deeper into debt until now he owed nearly two thousand rupees (two-hundred-and-sixty-six dollars). At best, there was little possibility of his ever accumulating such a staggering sum, but under his present circumstances it was plainly impossible. Out of desperation, he had sold his sewing machine, and a tailor without a sewing machine had no way to earn a living. He had come to Puttaparthi to ask Baba only for a sewing machine, but with the secret hope that Baba would give him the entire two thousand rupees.

"Sai Ram," Desai said to the tailor, as he continued on his way.

"Sai Ram," the tailor said.

As Desai passed the temporary shed with the dirt floor on his way toward the canteen he met another person he knew, a woman named Sukvarubhai, in her twenties, from Behar,

near Calcutta, who had established her temporary home in
the dirt next to where Desai had set up housekeeping. She
was small and pretty with soft Negroid features and a hole
in her left nostril where a jewel presumably had once been.
She wore a white sari of the cheapest cotton and twelve
pink glass bangles on her left wrist, six white ones on her
right. They had been on her wrist since her wedding
ceremony eleven years ago (it is considered inauspicious
to remove them). Six of the white ones had broken, a
misfortune she links with the fact that her husband left her
five years ago, placing her even lower on the social scale
than a widow, who, until Lord William Bentinck passed a
law against it in 1829, was expected to throw herself on her
husband's funeral pyre. This new law was such a severe violation of Indian belief it has been suggested by many histori-
ans that the ban of suttee by the British was one of the major
causes leading to the Indian revolt in 1857.

In the villages, though, while a widow is not expected to
kill herself, she is expected to conduct herself as if she were
dead, denying herself any pleasures and staying as much out
of sight as possible.

Because she had two children and no family to take care
of them, Sukvar could not quite disappear. She went to
work in a rice mill, earning barely enough to survive. She had
no hope of ever getting married again (men in Indian villages don't marry widows), and there was no hope whatsoever of working her way up to a better station in life. She
was determined, though, that her children would at least
have a chance, and the only way this could happen, she
knew, was if they somehow could manage to get an education.

One night she had a dream in which a holy man appeared
to her and said for her to bring the children to him. At that
time she did not know who Baba was and couldn't understand the dream, which she interpreted to be symbolic in

some way. But several months later, by chance, she happened to meet a stranger who had a picture of Baba. When
Sukvar saw the picture she recognized Baba as the man in her
dream. With no money at all she took her son, who was ten,
and her daughter, eight, and they started walking toward
Puttaparthi, which was over nine hundred miles away.

When she started on the trip she didn't know how far she
would have to go or even where Puttaparthi was, but with
complete conviction that she was meant to go and would
somehow get there she allowed no other thought to enter
her head.

Each time she and the children were hungry she knew she
would meet someone who would give them food and each
time she did. When they grew so tired they could walk no
farther she met a man who, after hearing her story, bought
her tickets on the train. For four days the passengers on the
train shared their food with her and the children until they
got off at the closest stop to Puttaparthi. There a bullock-
cart driver, after hearing her story, took up a collection
from the other bullock-cart drivers and bought her and the
children tickets on the bus.

It wasn't until she finally arrived at Puttaparthi that she
discovered Baba had a boarding school for boys at the
ashram, a fact which did not surprise her. She knew Baba
would take the children and the details of how were not of
great importance.

For three weeks she had been waiting for Baba to return
so that she could ask him to take the children. All the while
she lived on the generosity of strangers who gave, as she
received, with the feeling that it was Baba's will. The only
question she allowed herself to wonder about from time to
time was what Baba would do with her daughter, since the
school was only for boys; but she was not troubled by the
question, only curious.

"Did you hear about Kasturi's letter?" she asked Desai.

"Yes," he said. "I heard."

"If he is in Mysore then he'll have to . . ."

"Mysore? He's in Madras."

"No," she said. "I heard Mysore."

"Why should he be in Mysore? The tour was of Andhra."

"He got a call, I heard, from a devotee in Mysore. The governor, I think. Somebody important is dying."

"I didn't hear that."

"That's what I heard."

"The governor?"

"Somebody."

"I didn't hear that."

"Kasturi got a letter from him."

"I heard about the letter," Desai said, "but I heard he was in Madras."

"No. He's in Mysore."

"Maybe if he's in Mysore he'll have to go all the way back to Andhra to finish the tour."

"I don't think so," she said.

"At least he'll be here for Shivarathri," Desai said. "We know he'll be here for that."

She hesitated a few seconds as if debating whether to tell him or not.

"I had a dream last night," she said. "He came to me in a dream."

"Really?" This was news of considerable importance.

"Stop that!" she called to her son, who was about to throw a rock at a tree.

Desai turned to look over his shoulder at his own son, on his back. "He came to her in a dream."

The woman's son obeyed her reluctantly and she turned back to Desai. "He told me not to worry," she said. "He'll be here in two days he said."

"In the dream? He told you in the dream?"

" 'Tell everybody,' he told me. 'I'll be there in two days.' "

Desai had the uneasy feeling she was improvising but it was too important to ignore. He continued to the canteen, where he looked around, then went to one of the two tables, both made of unbroken slabs of charcoal-colored slate. The benches and the legs of the tables were also made of the same kind of slate, as were the floors, ceiling, and walls. The food was chopped and prepared on the slate floor of a tiny adjoining room, usually by three or four boys from the school who were temporarily assigned the duty under the supervision of an old lady. The canteen, which served only the simplest Indian meals, was never crowded. Almost all of the pilgrims, even the bachelors, cooked their own food. It was only for those few who for some reason could not cook, or could afford not to, that the ashram operated the cafe— usually at a loss and mainly to make it unnecessary for Baba's devotees to eat at the commercial establishments in the village, which overcharged and often served contaminated food.

Desai took his son from his back and sat him on the bench next to the only other person in the room, a merchant from Ceylon who was eating vegetable curry and rice with his fingers. Desai looked around for the waiter, but he was not in the room.

"Did you hear about Kasturi?" the merchant asked.

"Yes, but I just spoke to a woman, the woman with the two little children she wants to get in the school here, do you know who I mean?"

"No," the merchant said. "I just got here."

"Well, she had a dream last night. Baba came to her in a dream."

The merchant stopped eating. "Really?"

"He'll be here in two days, he told her. Tell everybody."

"Sai Ram," the merchant said.

"Sai Ram," Desai said, then he turned to his son, prompting the boy also to speak.

"Sai Ram," the boy said.

The merchant from Ceylon had been issued one of the rooms reserved for foreigners and important guests. These were for the most part one-room houses built by devotees for their own use but available to anyone the custodian chose to put in them when the owners were not in residence. One building, containing five separate units over the dormitory where the boys in Baba's school slept, had what was called a bathroom, which turned out to be exactly that, a room reserved exclusively for taking baths. There was no running water, no tub, no sink, only a hole in the wall which was supposed to serve as a drain for the water after it was splashed from the jug to the body. But the builder had neglected to slant the cement floor toward the hole so that whatever water spilled onto the floor stayed where it was spilled. There was also an uncovered hole in the floor that was intended to be used as a toilet, but it was neither connected to a cesspool nor any other system of drainage and the stench from the hole, which was constantly swarming with flies and mosquitoes, was unbearable for most people.

The merchant from Ceylon, however, was not in one of those rooms which were usually reserved for Americans and Europeans and those few distinguished Indians from cities who were used to private toilets.

The merchant had been given a room about six feet by four with a cement floor, no furniture, and no windows. He had come from Ceylon with his wife; two daughters, nine and seven; and two sons, twins, six months old. The twins were the reason for the trip, he told Desai.

"In 1967 I came here alone," he said. "It was September. A doctor friend of mine had been here and seen Baba and when he returned to his home in Ceylon, *vibhuthi* started dropping from the picture of Baba. It started from Baba's hand in the picture and soon the entire glass was covered with *vibhuthi*. I heard this and to clear my doubts I went to his house and I saw it. I put my finger on the ashes and tasted it. It tasted sweet and smelled like incense. Immediately I felt I had to come see Baba. For twenty years I had been looking for a guru. I am a Hindu and we believe it is important to find a master to guide you spiritually but everywhere I went, and I went to all the saints whenever I heard of one, I came away with doubts and not a good feeling. Anyway, that night, the night I saw Baba's picture with the *vibhuthi*, I went home and got a very high temperature and the following morning I made up my mind I had to come here to see him. It took me two weeks to get my passport and everything in order and then I went to the doctor, my friend, and asked him for the address of Baba and he gave me the details and the proper route to take to come here. So I came alone and I waited the first day but I was not called for an interview with Baba and not the second day and I began to grow impatient and angry. I had come so far, why did he not see me? However, I stayed there in front of the temple and I took no meals and only when I felt too weak then I went to the canteen for milk, but even at night I stayed there on the ground in front of the temple. On the third day in the morning, about seven-thirty, Baba came out of his door and he motioned to me with his finger and I went to his private room, and when I got there he told me before I could say a word that I had come so far from Ceylon and that for twenty years I had been looking for a guru and then he waved his hand and took some *vibhuthi* from the air and he put some on my forehead between my eyes with his thumb. When I saw him waving his hand I felt the whole room turning. I forgot to say that while I was waiting in the room, I saw in the photograph of Baba—you know, the big one on the floor in the corner—I saw my girls, my two children. They were green-colored. Then Baba came into the room where I was taken and Baba was standing there just smiling and then I was taken to the small place on the stairs, where he gives the private interviews sometimes, and Baba asked me not to worry for anything. He said I have trouble at home but when I go back there everything will be all right. I was weeping. He said 'Don't cry like a lady,' and he gave me about eleven or twelve packets of *vibhuthi*. Each had a different taste and a different color but most of them smelled of camphor, a strong smell. My wife had so many illnesses. I applied the *vibhuthi* to my wife, and to my friends who were ailing, and they got well. But back to Baba. Then he took this ring from the air and he put it on my finger and it fit my finger perfectly, as you can see, and he said 'Don't remove it, don't ever remove it. Whenever you want something, concentrate on this ring and it will happen.'

"Well, I purchased pictures of Baba from the book stall, about thirty or forty, and I distributed them to my friends. I put one picture at the altar where I do puja and one day at two in the afternoon I saw these holy ashes and some sandal-wood liquid paste on the picture. Some came from the mouth of the picture and I thought the children had done something and I didn't take it seriously, but more and more *vibhuthi* began falling from the picture and I took the picture from the puja room and put it on the table. And from that day, which was nearly three months ago, *vibhuthi* has been coming constantly on the picture. After two weeks, I saw water drops, which stayed two or three weeks under the glass, between the glass and the picture. Then one day I was washing my shrine room when I noticed a projection coming out of the floor and I saw holy ashes coming out of the floor in the shape of a lingam. They are still coming.

Well, I performed prayers to that lingam and my friends came to see this because they could not believe it and the color started to change and it became rose-colored.

"But one more thing I must tell you. After my interview that first time with Baba I was in Madras, where I had to spend the night before catching the airplane the next day, and I was in this small inn. At about two in the morning I heard noise and I woke up and I saw two or three people trying to gain entrance through the window and I called out for the boy in charge but there was no response so I called Baba. I don't know why. It happened automatically. And I started repeating his name perhaps a hundred times and then I felt sleepy and even though I was frightened I fell asleep and I don't know if I saw this in my sleep as a dream or some kind of hallucination or what it was, but I saw suddenly four armed guards, one in each corner of my room, and I felt they were standing there guarding me all night, and in the morning when I woke up I saw the last one just before he faded away. At six in the morning, I told the manager of the inn, but he said it never happened. But I know it did. Another thing that same day—there were no vacant seats on the airplane and I had only three rupees left with me which would not have been enough for a room at the inn and to take food. I didn't know what to do, so I asked Baba what I should do and he told me, that is I felt him saying to me, 'Go to the airport, wait there, you will get a seat.' So I went to the airport and five minutes before the airplane was to leave they told me one person didn't show up and I had my seat.

"The reason I have come here now is for the ceremony when babies are given their first solid food. I forgot to tell you, my wife had five miscarriages and we wanted a son very badly and Baba told me in the interview 'Don't worry, you will have a son' and look what he has given me, two sons—twins! And I promised before they were born if I got a son I would take him here and ask Baba to feed him this first rice feeding of solid food, so that is why I am here, to bless my children."

"I was a devotee of Shirdi," Desai said.

"Really?" the merchant said, impressed.

"In 1956," Desai said, "I heard about this Sai Baba and I was curious to see him."

"You will see him. You will see him," the merchant said.

"Oh, I saw him," Desai said. "In 1960 I had taken the boy to many doctors for treatment, but no one could do anything, of course, so when I came to know about Baba I thought I should come here but I had very little faith and didn't feel able to make the long journey from Bombay, where I came from. But in 1965 I heard that Baba was coming to Bombay and I had heard of a man who had a picture of Baba and *vibhuthi* was coming on it so I went to see it, but I didn't go to see Baba when he was there. I was a devotee of Shirdi and I didn't like anyone claiming to be him. Then in 1966 I began to feel something special for Baba in my heart, and, let me see, February, I remember, I took a vow to stop seeing films because I read in a book that Baba did not approve of the cinema. Then one day that year Baba came again to Bombay. This was in 1966. It was about ten forty-five in the morning and Baba appeared on the balcony. I was there with two friends and the moment I saw him I burst into tears, I don't know why but it was Lord Krishna standing there, I knew, I could feel it. I closed my eyes. I couldn't speak. It was the most profound moment I ever felt in my life.

"That year in December I came here with my wife and my son and finally we got an interview and when I got there with Baba finally, I couldn't speak. I opened my mouth and no words came out. He told me everything. He told me I was a devotee of Shirdi, he told me about the day I had seen him in Bombay and how I had cried. I couldn't believe it, I fell at his feet. He touched me on the head and said, 'Don't worry, worship God.' Then he gave me some oil for the boy to put on his legs and he gave a bottle of the same tonic to my wife, she had high blood pressure, but she hadn't told him anything about that. He told her to take the tonic, it would be good for her nervousness. We wondered later how the same tonic could be good for polio and high blood pressure but he told her to take the tonic, and so for two days my wife took the tonic, then on the third day she didn't take it. On the fourth day we were called by Baba and he said why did she stop taking the medicine? He also told me to stop smoking and we went back to our home. The next year I lost my wife, but I felt Baba's presence the night she died. I could feel that he had come there in his presence to bless her when she left the body and I felt him tell me, 'worship God' just as he told me the first time I saw him. I came again to Puttaparthi that year for Baba's birthday in November, and when I had my interview he said, 'Leave everything to me, don't worry. Take the boy home,' he said, 'and bring him back in February for Shivarathri.' So we have come back."

"Yes, yes," the merchant said.

"I am here to follow Baba's instruction," Desai said. "Let him do what he wants. I can't tell you the feeling he gives me. When I was five years old I lost my mother and have the same love for him now as for a mother. There is nothing more in this life. He will make my son walk, I know he will because he said he would."

The waiter came into the room and over to their table, to take their order. He was twenty-seven, but looked no more than fourteen.

"Do you know Baba cured him of polio?" Desai asked the merchant.

"Sai Ram," the merchant said.

"Tell him," Desai said to the waiter. "Tell him the story."

The waiter, whose name was Eswaria Narsia, spoke in a soft whisper with a sweet gentleness which seemed woven entirely from the fabric of a quiet, almost ecstatic peace.

He was born in a village about a hundred and fifty miles from Puttaparthi, he said, the only son of a very poor farmer. He had three sisters. When he was three years old his mother died.

"Show him your legs," Desai said, impatient to get to the good part.

The waiter lifted his dhoti, which was draped from his waist to his ankles, revealing his thin legs which obviously had once been stricken with polio.

"Did you see him walk?" Desai asked the merchant. "Walk," he said to the waiter.

Self-consciously, but eager to demonstrate his love for Baba, the waiter walked across the small room and back.

"Did you see? He doesn't limp," Desai said. "He doesn't even limp."

"Sai Ram," the merchant said.

"I was twenty years old when I first came to Baba," the waiter said. "I had heart weakness and polio and some friends of my father told him about Baba and we thought about coming and we talked about it and then my father decided to take me, so one morning, I think it was about four o'clock in the morning, he walked to the next village with me on his back and we took the train. We stayed all afternoon and all night on the train and then we waited for the bus and after the bus we took the bullock cart to Putta-parthi, only to find out when we got here that Baba was not here. So we waited one day after another, never knowing when he would be here but we had come and so for twelve days we waited. Then when he came my father carried me and we both slept near the temple and we stayed there all day and all night only leaving to take food and to go to the fields. For days, I don't remember how many, Baba would come in the evening and I was lying near the temple and my father would help me sit up. When Baba came near me I was very happy, but there were hundreds of people waiting. And then one day Baba came and stood near me and Baba asked Kasturi, 'Who is this boy?' and Kasturi told him my name and the village where I came from and Baba told me, very sweet, I could touch his feet and I did and I felt very happy and then Baba materialized *vibhuthi* in his hand and he gave it to me in my hand and he said, 'Eat this. Tomorrow I'll see you.' So we waited all the next day at the temple and in the evening, about six-thirty, Baba came out and he said to my father to bring me to the interview room. So my father carried me inside the temple to the interview room and then Baba, when he finished with other people, came to me and he let me touch his feet. Then he said to my father, 'Darasara festival will be here soon and many thousands of people will be coming and you won't get a place to stay and it will be raining and you will not be comfortable, so you take the boy back to your village for one month.' He gave my father a package of *vibhuthi* and he said, 'Give this to the boy in water every morning and every evening and apply it to his legs.' And then to me he said I must say Sai Ram day and night. Every day. Every night. All day and all night. I must go to sleep with God's name on my lips and wake up with his name on my lips and all day think of nothing else.

"So we went back to the village and I felt a little improvement. I thought I could feel something in my legs. Before I could never feel anything in my legs. Well, three months later we came back with my eldest sister and this time we brought nothing with us. But this time Baba told my father to stay here with me. We stayed one year and slowly I started improving. I could feel in my legs. And every now and again Baba would give me *vibhuthi* and I would go to sing *bhajans* and I said Sai Ram all day. That's all I did, over and over. 'Sai Ram.' 'Sai Ram.' And Baba told my father to carry me around the temple three times in the morning and three times in the evening and he would, and then I started walking, or trying to walk, with my father on one side holding me up and my sister holding me up on the other side and they tried to teach me how to walk, moving my legs for me. And then one day Baba came out on the balcony and he shouted down to my father and my sister, 'Don't hold him!' and he yelled for me to start walking and I did. I started walking alone with a stick. This was nine o'clock in the morning and several hundred people were here and they saw it and Baba walked back into his room and everybody crowded around me and my father asking what happened and talking about the miracle and my father told them what happened, those who didn't see it, and there was much excitement.

"The next month Baba called me again for an interview and he told my father and sister to go and leave me here and they did. I slept in the old temple yard in the village and I ate in the canteen, and for three months I would go around the temple three times in the morning and three times in the evening and all day long I said 'Sai Ram,' 'Sai Ram' to myself.

"I had nothing to do with myself so I used to come to the canteen and give water to the people eating here.

"After one year my father and sister came back to ask Baba to let me come home just for the wedding of my youngest sister and Baba said all right. Then after the wedding they brought me back to Puttaparthi and Baba told me to work in the canteen."

Tears had come to the waiter's eyes. He stopped a moment to swallow and to wipe his eyes.

"I want to stay here the rest of my life," he said, "because Baba is God. Anyone can see that. Just look at my legs. And every year they are growing stronger and bigger."

"Does he see you now?" the merchant asked. "How often does he see you?"

"Now," the waiter said, "now Baba sees me only every six or eight months, but if I need clothes, he gives me clothes with his own hands or through the canteen manager, and if I need money for anything it isn't even necessary to tell him. As soon as I need it somebody comes from Baba and they give me money."

"He will cure you too," Desai said to his son. "Do you believe it? Tell me you believe it."

"I believe it," the son said, not believing it.

A short fat man with a blue dacron shirt over his dhoti came in.

"Did you hear about the letter?" the man said.

"Kasturi's letter?" Desai asked.

"No," the man said. "Another man got a letter from his wife in Hyderabad and she said she heard Baba was there now and would stay there for Shivarathri."

"Hyderabad?" the merchant said.

"Impossible," Desai said.

"How could he not be here for Shivarathri?" the waiter said.

"He's there right now," the man said.

"In Hyderabad?" Desai said.

"I heard it from the man himself who got the letter from his wife."

❧ SIX

Baba was not in Hyderabad. At about seven o'clock the night before he had arrived at his house in Whitefield, the residential community just outside of Bangalore where the writer had first met him. It originally had been a maharaja's summer palace but a few years ago it was bought by an industrialist, a devotee of Baba's, and turned over to Baba for his exclusive use.

The estate, which covers five acres, was surrounded by a cement fence which had once been painted white. Just inside the heavy, elaborate, wrought-iron gate was a small house where Mr. Dixit, the caretaker, lived with his wife. He had been a devotee of Shirdi and came to challenge Baba nearly twenty years ago, at which time Baba not only told him intimate details of his life and experiences with Shirdi but also materialized out of the air a photograph of Shirdi Dixit had taken and then lost years before. At that moment Dixit, shaken by the experience, asked Baba if he could stay with him and serve him the rest of his life. Baba laughed. "I told you once at Shirdi," Baba said, "you must learn to tend your gates, meaning the gates of your soul, of course, but later, some time in the future, we shall deal with that."

When Baba was presented with the house at Whitefield he called Dixit to him and said, "Now you can tend my gates as well as your own. I told you you would be a gate-keeper."

Inside the main gate about halfway down a long dirt driveway was an enormous banyan tree, hundreds of years old, with dozens of snakelike roots intertwining and overlapping on the fitted circular ledge which formed a pedestal for the tree. Under the tree was a thronelike chair. At the end of the driveway was the main house behind another elaborate wrought-iron gate.

The two-story house, painted dark green, looked as if it had been built in the thirties by an architect who was instructed to come up with something semitropical but modern and felt obligated to use all the abstract, stainless steel, kidney-shaped innovations he could remember after a quick guided tour through Radio City.

By eight o'clock in the morning hundreds of people were waiting alongside of the dirt driveway, the men on one side of the road, the women on the other. Many had been there all night, having somehow gotten the news that Baba was coming, in this case even before Dixit had found out. No one has ever been able to figure out how the news spreads so quickly and so accurately when Baba is due to arrive someplace, but each time people are already waiting to catch sight of him before he gets there.

Among those waiting were young men, young women, old men and women, women with babies in their arms, and one middle-aged man (the only person there in a Western-style business suit) in a wheel chair. Also in a wheel chair was a mongoloid child. Her sad-faced mother, in her twenties, waited silently beside her. There was no talk, no movement of any kind.

A few minutes after eight an Indian-made Ambassador

sedan drove through the gates and parked near the banyan tree. Dr. Gokok was in the back seat with the writer, who had arrived in Bangalore the night before.

The writer had gotten all of the information he could from everybody he could find at Puttaparthi who knew Baba and would agree to speak about him. From time to time he would hear from Kasturi or by mail from one of the devotees in Bangalore that Baba was rumored to be at one town or another at some specific date, and each time the writer had made every effort to contact him. The first time, hearing that Baba might be staying with a certain man in Madras, the writer asked a permanent resident at the ashram how he should address the telegram he planned to send.

"Why do you have to send a telegram?" the devotee wanted to know. "He knows where you are and what you're thinking."

"I know," the writer said, "but just to satisfy my own impatience."

"Just send it to God," she said.

"No address?"

"Just God. Madras, if you want to."

On his way to the telegraph office the writer stopped at Kasturi's house to get the exact address of the man in Madras.

He might just as well have sent the telegram to God in care of The Universe. There was no reply from Baba or from any of his aides, not to that telegram or to any of the others he sent.

Finally, the writer decided, enough was enough. There was no hope of his being able to document anything about Baba with anything resembling scientific accuracy. He had come with the idea of irrefutably proving many of the claims he had heard about Baba. Now he didn't know what to write. He had seen enough and heard enough to realize the only thing he knew with any degree of certainty was that he had to get away from Puttaparthi. So he called for a taxi in Bangalore to come to get him. If he had to wait for Baba, he would wait at what passed for a luxury hotel in the relative comfort and sanity of a city. If Baba didn't show up in three or four days, to hell with the book. He was going home.

He called Gokok as soon as he got to the hotel.

"I was just trying to reach you," Gokok said, "but the telephone at Puttaparthi is out of order."

"Have you heard from Baba?"

"He's here. In Bangalore. He just arrived a few minutes ago."

"Can I see him today?"

"No. He has some business matters today and tonight he takes food with the governor, but in the morning, at last, I'll take you to see him."

The writer got very little sleep that night.

"I'll only be a moment," Gokok said when they stopped near Baba's house at Whitefield. As Gokok got out of the car he indicated the writer should wait there. Then Gokok went to the wrought-iron gate near the house and attracted the attention of an aide inside who seemed very glad to see him.

The writer got out of the car and looked at the people beside the road. He did not see the young Indian man in a white shirt and wide white pants until he spoke.

"May I ask your good name, sir, and the purpose of your mission in India?"

This was the standard question asked of most foreigners in all parts of India, and rather than go into the complicated reasons of why he was there the writer found it simpler to say he was a tourist, which always seemed to delight the Indians, who took great pride in the idea that their country was worth traveling thousands of miles to see, even if they couldn't quite comprehend why anyone would want to bother.

"I am here with this letter, you see," the young man said, showing the writer an airmail letter he had written on the kind of paper which when folded becomes its own envelope. "I am writing to a company in Canada, hoping to obtain from them employment. But before I send the letter, if I could only get Baba to bless it, to touch it, I know my prayers for this employment would be answered."

The writer was annoyed with himself for not being interested, but he had had all the blind faith he could handle.

At this point he looked up and saw (in an irrational instant of panic) that all of the people who had been waiting beside the road were now coming toward him. A second later he realized they were not coming to him at all but toward the banyan tree. They sat on the ground around the tree, the men on one side, the women on the other, and started to sing *bhajans,* the same ones which were sung at Puttaparthi. After a few minutes Gokok came back to the car.

"He'll be coming out in a minute," Gokok said and before he finished saying it, Baba appeared through the gates.

Three devotees followed him at a respectful distance. Two were in their sixties or seventies, one seemed to be in his thirties.

Baba stopped to inspect the foundation of a building that was being laid between the main house and the banyan tree. All of the workmen stopped what they were doing as he approached.

Looking at a holy man, just being allowed to see him, is one of the three ways to receive his blessing, the Hindus believe, and is so cherished an honor that it is not unusual for devotees to wait days, even weeks, just to be able to glance at a holy man for a few seconds as he steps into or out of a car or crosses in front of a window. To be blessed by seeing him is called taking *darsan*. To be allowed to touch his feet is called *sparsan*, and is of course a much more fervently sought-after blessing. To hear him speak, *sambhasana*, is the greatest blessing of all.

The writer followed Gokok to where Baba was talking to the workmen. When Baba saw Gokok he greeted him with warm affection, spontaneously hugging him and patting him soundly on the back.

"Do you have the list of supplies we need for the laboratory?" Baba asked in Telugu.

Gokok took a sheet of paper from his jacket pocket. "Yes. Yes," he said in Telugu. "I have all the information."

"Good," Baba said in English. "Good."

He still had not looked at the writer, nor did Gokok make any effort to include him in the conversation. Baba began talking about the tour he had just finished.

"In one place," Baba said in Telugu, "over three hundred thousand people showed up, mostly communists. Three hundred thousand! But they were very quiet. The chairman said he had never seen them so quiet. I also gave a talk at the Lions' Club." He laughed at the idea of naming a club for an animal.

"The lion means intelligence," Baba said, "reason. And the mind is the elephant which is under the control of the lion, or should be. I also spoke to a convention of doctors." He seemed irritated at this memory. "They're ruining the world, the doctors," Baba continued. "They give people pills to not have babies so they can jump on each other like wild dogs. Instead of wasting all that money on birth control they ought to spend that money on food. I told the chairman that, who was also a doctor, and the chairman agreed with me."

The people under the tree were still singing and abruptly Baba started walking toward them. As he walked he held his left arm behind his back and made a series of continuous motions with the fingers of his right hand as if, it appeared, he were testing the air to see how heavy it was or what it contained. Wherever he is, whatever he is doing, he continues to finger the air constantly. The gesture, he later explained, was his means of communicating with devotees and their problems all over the world.

"At the moment we are sitting here," he later told the writer, "you think I am talking only to you, but my fingers are dealing with problems everywhere."

His fingers also can read the hundreds of letters which come to him each week from all over the world, Baba claimed. Even though he cannot speak or read most of the languages the letters are written in, he is able to tell what the letters are about simply by feeling them, and in most cases is able to handle their problems telepathically. If an answer is required, Baba directs one of his helpers, usually Kasturi, to write the letter, but he goes through all of the mail he receives himself. Every letter goes through his fingers.

When Baba reached the crowd, still singing under the banyan tree, many tried to touch his feet. He allowed this privilege to certain people and to others, for some reason, he would not. The three devotees who served as his aides on this walk gently motioned for the crowd to remain seated and not to try to approach Baba now. Nevertheless, a few people offered him flowers, some of which he accepted, immediately handing them to one of the aides.

The singing continued as he made his way to the chair under the tree, having stopped at one point to speak with a very old man in a wheel chair. Baba pushed up the sleeve on his right arm until it was above the elbow, then he held his right hand out, palm down, the fingers spread apart, and after a slow, rotating motion closed his fingers. When he turned his hand over and opened the fingers, his palm was covered with *vibhuthi*. Gently he spread the ashes on the old man's neck and throat.

Baba stopped again beside a young man holding a girl about six in his arms. Again he materialized some *vibhuthi* in his hand and rubbed some of it on the girl's forehead, putting the rest of the ashes into her mouth. Then he rubbed her neck with both hands, vigorously, and continued toward the tree, stopping again when a middle-aged man stood up and whispered something to Baba.

Baba materialized more *vibhuthi* and transferred it from his hand to the man's hand. Then Baba went to the chair under the tree where he sat for a time listening to the singing, apparently very pleased.

At one point he started conducting the singers with his hand, then he started clapping to the rhythm of the song, urging the others to begin clapping also. When they all were clapping to the rhythm of the beat, Baba got up and went toward the women's section. He stopped at the mongoloid child, materialized some more *vibhuthi*, and put part of it on her forehead, the rest on her throat. From time to time, as he walked among the group of women, he would stop to allow one or two to touch his feet—but generally he discouraged this. Many women held notes up to him. Each one he accepted he passed on to one of his aides, after holding it for an instant as if to find out what the note contained without having to bother looking at it.

The young aide carried a towel which he handed to Baba each time he materialized *vibhuthi*. Baba wiped his hands clean, then returned the towel before going on to someone else.

When Baba completed the circle around the tree he started back toward the house. The writer and Gokok followed him.

On the way Baba stopped at a young man, a spastic, seated in a regular straight-back chair, who asked Baba for *vibhuthi*.

"No," Baba said, then he pointed to the young man's heart.

"In your heart," Baba said, "in your heart. Have faith in your heart."

As Baba turned to go the young man bent down, futilely trying to touch Baba's feet. Seeing this, Baba lifted his foot so that the young man could touch it. Then he went in through the gate past a group of people who had been selected for private interviews, all of whom were sitting on the ground outside a side entrance.

Gokok and the writer followed Baba in through the front door to a screened-in porch. About a dozen people were seated there, the men on one side, the women on the other.

As Baba went from the porch inside the house to the main reception room, Gokok and the writer sat on the floor at the end of the line near the door. Most of the people waiting were Indian. The men all wore Western-style clothes, the women all wore saris. There was only one Westerner, a fat, middle-aged man with a shaved head and a thick black mustache, who the writer later discovered was a businessman from California.

Only one piece of furniture was on the porch, a flamingo-pink leather couch against the wall, left of the entrance. On the cushion of the sofa and propped against the wall was a gold-framed, life-size, tinted photograph of Baba. Draped around the frame were several garlands of fresh flowers.

Other photos of Baba in different poses were on the wall. In one he was riding an elephant, in one he was riding a pony.

On each side of the door leading to the reception room inside the house was a waist-high porcelain elephant, its trunk wrapped around a cornucopia. Over the door was a mounted tiger's head.

Presently Baba returned to the porch, where he sat in the middle of the floor at the far end, near the pink sofa. The writer noticed that while he somehow gave the impression of being stocky, upon closer examination he was seen to have thin arms and legs but just the suggestion of a pot belly. His face was round and full with, again, only the suggestion of a double chin.

So far Baba still had given no indication of having seen the writer or of being aware in any way of his presence.

For a time Baba talked in Telugu about the need to worship God and lead the pure life. "Four things are necessary to cook rice," he said. "The rice, a pot, water, and fire; but even the finest rice in the purest water in the most expensive pot cannot be cooked without the fire."

At one point an elderly lady came in. Baba greeted her warmly and motioned for her to take a seat with the women. She was the governor's wife, whose daughter was in another room with a group of students waiting for an interview with Baba.

Then Baba began speaking in Kannada to one of the women, alternating with side comments to one of the men in Telugu, and then he turned to the Californian with the shaved head.

"Your Mahesh Yogi," Baba said, refusing to call the Maharishi of Beatles fame a Maharishi, which is a higher title than Yogi. "I call him your yogi because you Americans invented him. Well, he sent his two American messengers to arrange an interview with me, but I said he is lower than the lowest student. Let him come and sit outside with the others. We cannot accept that, you know, when a holy man begins to charge money. It becomes an exhibition, like a circus. He did serious harm in America, becoming associated with hippies and making ridiculous promises. He is like a man who gives a cat boiling milk and the cat burns its tongue. The next time somebody offers the cat milk he will run away."

The Maharishi was speaking in Bangalore that day, which is what prompted Baba's tirade. For a time he continued speaking to the American in Telugu, with Gokok translating into English, but at one point in a story Baba was telling he interrupted Gokok, correcting his translation.

"No, no, not goat. Donkey," Baba said. "It is better to have one spoon of cow's milk than a gallon of milk from a donkey."

Meanwhile the singing from under the banyan tree continued and Baba, in connection with a point he was making about how right words lead to right thinking which leads to right action, began telling a parable which Gokok translated.

"Rama said go listen to the sheep and tell me what they say," Gokok translated. "They saw kids on one side and mothers on the other calling to each other, 'baa baa . . .' "

"Not 'baa baa,' " Baba said, correcting Gokok. " 'Maa!' 'Baa Baa' is my name."

" 'Baa' is what sheep say in America," Gokok said.

"These are not American sheep," Baba said. "These are Indian sheep."

He then explained that the word "maa" sounds like the word for "my" in Telugu, and the point of the story was that one should never say "my" or "mine." Sheep say that and man should be on a higher level than sheep.

Suddenly, with no comment or transition, Baba got up and crossed to the far end of the porch, which was empty. Immediately he was joined by nine men and one woman. When Gokok got up to join the group, his leg had fallen asleep. Baba laughed.

"You live too well in chairs," Baba said, and then he started rubbing Gokok's leg to stimulate the circulation.

Abruptly, as if they were continuing exactly where they might have left off perhaps weeks ago, the group plunged into a meeting which was conducted partly in English, mostly in Telugu, about the college Baba was building. One of the purposes of the meeting was to compile a list of everything that would be required physically, including the specific books that would be needed. Then one of the businessmen brought up the point of whether the college should be at Whitefield or in Bangalore, discussing the various tax advantages of each. It was finally decided that the committee would continue exploring the various aspects of this problem, but Baba cautioned them not to deliberate too long. A principal had been engaged to begin work six months from now, he announced.

During the meeting the young devotee who had followed Baba with the towel came to him with a small silver box that he gave to Baba, who opened it, revealing several smaller silver boxes inside. From one of the silver boxes Baba took several betel leaves and in a tiny silver bowl found a small brush that he used to spread a thick amount of pink paste onto the leaves, which he then folded and put into his mouth.

This was the first time the writer had seen anyone taking pan, and he was not yet aware that in India pan was as common as cigarettes. When he asked the young man who brought the box what the pink stuff was, he was told it was pure calcium. Later Gokok told the writer it was pink-colored lime.

Baba ate about half a dozen leaves, occasionally eating them with tiny palm nuts. From time to time he would wipe his face and eyes and mouth with the small hand towel the young man had given him.

After about ten minutes Baba suddenly got up, ending the meeting. As the members of the committee gathered together in groups of two and three to discuss the problems among themselves, Baba looked at the writer for the first time. When their eyes met the writer felt as if the breath had been knocked out of him. His ears started ringing. He felt completely disoriented. When Baba looked away the ringing stopped.

Baba turned to put his arm around Gokok and led him to a corner of the porch where they could talk in private. Without looking at the writer Baba went inside the house to the reception room and from there into one of the small rooms used for private interviews.

When Gokok joined the writer he seemed embarrassed and for a moment unable to say what he had to say.

"He wants me to bring you back tonight to have food with him," Gokok said. "And then tomorrow," he said, "you can go back to America."

Dr. Gokok at Baba's left. *John Worldlie*

Students at Baba's school at Prasanthi Nilayam. *John Worldlie*

Baba's elephant putting a garland of flowers around his neck.

Baba presiding at a special ceremony. *Studio Sai-Datta*

Baba in his living quarters.

Baba materializing *vibhuthi* for a devotee. *John Worldlie*

🌱 SEVEN

Asha arrived at Puttaparthi just before sunset. She had taken a taxi from the airport at Bangalore, having told the driver where she wanted to go without knowing exactly where it was. The driver didn't know either and repeatedly, throughout most of the hundred and twenty-seven miles, had to stop to ask the way, mostly of people who gave directions that turned out to be wrong.

On the way they passed aspects of India she had never seen before: A tribe of nomads; tiny villages composed of half a dozen straw houses in the middle of vast stretches of red clay, sterile, dehydrated earth out of which nothing could grow; small clusters of people squatting for no apparent reason by the side of the road (resting? waiting to see the one car which might pass every hour?); ancient ruins of walls and shrines that would be considered priceless treasures of antiquity almost anywhere else, but were merely useless here, their original purpose forgotten long ago. And the monkeys, always the monkeys, in the middle of the road, on the side of the road, in the trees beside the road. Once when the driver stopped to relieve himself, a small nervous monkey jumped through the window into the front seat of the car.

Asha didn't actually scream but her call to the driver revealed far more hysteria than she intended. He had crossed the road to a ditch some distance away and when he heard her he came hurrying back, trying to button his fly as he ran. When he saw the monkey he laughed and gently chased the monkey away.

When she arrived at Puttaparthi the back of her sari was thoroughly soaked with perspiration, her mouth dry, and her teeth were coated with a layer of gritty dust from the road. As they drove in through the main gate they saw a group of perhaps a hundred women who had formed a bucket brigade, passing jugfuls of water from hand to hand from the ashram well near the main gate all the way up to the hospital at the top of a small rocky hill.

The driver got out of the taxi and went to the village for tea. Asha began looking for the custodian, whose name was Suryaprakasarao but who, she knew, was called Surayya. Her aunt had gotten the information from her friend who called her friend who called the man who knew about Baba and Asha was told to find the custodian when she got to Puttaparthi and he would help her. She had not thought to notify him in advance that she was coming. When she finally found him (a tall, skinny, S-shaped man in his seventies, wearing, as all the men there did, a short-sleeved shirt over a dhoti and no shoes), she did not know exactly what to say to him. Finally, without telling him her name, she mentioned the name of the friend of her aunt's friend.

"You are from Delhi, isn't it?" Surayya asked.

"Did somebody tell you I was coming?" she asked.

"No," he said. "Your manner of dress, the way you speak, your hand luggage."

"When will I be able to see Baba?" she asked him.

"Baba is not here," Surayya said.

"Where is he?"

Surayya laughed. "Nobody knows."

"Can you find out?" she asked. "Can you telephone or telegraph someone? I'll pay for it, of course."

"Nobody knows where he is," Surayya said.

She hadn't paid the driver, she remembered, and the taxi was still there, so she could go back with him to Bangalore. As she considered whether to stay or to leave, Surayya went into a small stone building marked "Police."

Asha looked around. Nothing green could be seen in any direction, only dust and miles of parched earth. For a moment, she had a terrible longing for the tiny patch of grass around her apartment, which, even as she thought of it, seemed strange to her. She had not until then been aware of liking grass especially, or, in fact, even noticing it. If anything she and her husband had always made fun of their pathetic little excuse for a lawn.

Surayya came out of the house with a large number of keys on a huge ring.

"You can stay in this room for a few days," he said. "The owner is coming for Shivarathri, but you will be comfortable there, I think, until he gets here."

She was not aware of what a rare privilege she had been given. Except foreigners, almost everyone else who arrived at Puttaparthi had to take care of his own living accommodations. Apparently she gave the impression of being a foreigner, she later decided, even though she wore a sari, and, on her forehead, between her eyes, a *tika* (the red paste mark which in ancient times was used to denote caste but is now used purely cosmetically the way Western women use lipstick).

Surayya led her up the steps of a building at one end of the compound to a screened porch, where he unlocked one of the five rooms usually reserved for Americans.

"Here is the key," he said after opening an enormous padlock on the door. "Whenever you go out of the room, make sure the lock is on. There are people from the village who come into the compound when no one is looking to steal."

The room, which was the size her closet had been in England, had bare concrete floors and walls. Hanging from a beam under the exposed roof was a naked twenty-watt light bulb which, Surayya explained, was not functioning because when Baba was away they did not use electricity. It was too expensive.

Surayya took her into the other room, the bathroom, and deciding she would not know how to use the toilet any more than the Americans did, he picked up the earthenware jug near the hole in the floor and splashed some water into the hole demonstrating how one should attempt to flush it. The stench nauseated Asha, and she quickly went back into the front room where the smell was only a little less disturbing.

"If there is anything you want, please intimate your needs," Surayya said. "There is a canteen in the compound. Baba does not want you to eat in the village outside. Those fellows are not clean and many of them will charge you too much as well."

Then Surayya was gone, leaving her in the dark room which had no furniture, not even a mat to sleep on, she noticed. She knew it was customary to travel with one's own bedding in India, but she had made the trip too impulsively, she decided, to have thought anything through properly. Somehow, illogically, she realized she had expected something on the order of a Hilton hotel.

As she stood there wondering what to do, a very pretty Indian girl, about nineteen, came to the open door and knocked.

"Excuse me," the young girl said. "Can I help you in any way?"

Asha accepted the girl's invitation to sit down a moment in the girl's room next door. It was simply but adequately furnished with a straw cot covered by a mosquito net, a dark blue armchair, a large photograph of Baba on the wall over an altar for worship—on which were several smaller pictures of Baba, a candle, incense, and flowers carefully arranged in front of each picture.

Asha looked at Baba's picture a moment, not having expected him to look like that at all, and then, at the girl's invitation, sat down in the armchair, while the girl sat on a straw mat on the floor.

The girl was painfully shy, explaining with considerable difficulty that since she had become a devotee of Baba's, she no longer seemed able to make casual conversation. Her father was a maharaja who also was a devotee of Baba's, and she had come to spend a few weeks before and after Shiva-rathri, hoping to be able to see Baba at a distance once or twice a day, which would be enough for her. She no longer needed private interviews or special attention. Just to see him was enough to put her in a state of perfect peace.

When she discovered that Asha had never seen Baba and indeed knew very little about him, she was reluctant to speak of him and yet eager to help Asha cope with the doubts that she so obviously felt about being there.

"I was educated in England," the young girl said, "as you were, apparently, from your accent. And I know how foolish it must sound for me to say it, but you will find out for yourself when you see him. As soon as you see him you will feel it. He will tell you everything about yourself and you will see how quickly your doubts will disappear."

Suddenly the loud voice of an American shattered the hushed atmosphere around them, and Asha realized for the first time they had been whispering.

"If you put something on the fucking fire it'll burn," the man said.

"I know it'll burn," a woman said.

"Well take it off," the man said.

"Americans," the maharaja's daughter explained. "In the room next to yours."

Footsteps were heard on the porch and the taxi driver, looking for Asha, walked past the open doorway without having seen her inside.

"I think he's looking for me," Asha said, getting up.

The driver had gone to Asha's room, number seven, where Surayya said he would find her, and he was inside, examining the bathroom, when she came in.

"These are really nice," the driver said. "My brother has a house like this, but he's very rich. He owns a silk shop on Mahatma Gandhi Road."

Asha looked around, knowing she had now arrived at the point of no return. Once the driver left she was stuck here with no apparent way of getting out, unless she called a taxi in Bangalore to come and get her and that would take at least five hours, assuming, of course, there was a telephone somewhere at the ashram, an assumption which in no way seemed at all certain from what she had seen so far. Nevertheless, she paid the driver and took the phone number of the taxi company in Bangalore so that she could call him to come get her when she was ready to leave.

She went out to the porch with the driver and watched him walk down the steps and to the taxi, which he had parked by the house.

He waved good-by and called to her, assuring her he would come get her personally the minute she called the office. Then he got in the car and drove off.

She stood a moment watching the dust the car stirred up, then she felt someone's presence on the porch and turned to see a woman about four feet ten, her strong, chunky little body reminding Asha immediately of Lucy in the comic strip "Peanuts," which an American friend regularly sent her.

"I'm Jayalakshmi," she said, "the doctor here, at the hospital up there."

The doctor was about fifty Asha eventually decided from the bits and pieces of her life she mentioned here and there, but she looked in her late thirties. A pair of horn-rimmed glasses with unusually thick lenses magnified her mischievous eyes, giving her the look of a snarly pixie. The snarl, one quickly learned, was an acquired characteristic.

She was a licensed doctor, trained in London, but the whole idea of medicine was a joke to her. What need could there possibly be for medicine when a living avatar existed on this planet? The hospital was built, she said, for those of little faith and she would dutifully set a broken leg or give a shot of penicillin, but she was absolutely convinced there could be no cure unless Baba willed it—and if he willed it what was the need for all those expensive medications?

"He puts you to the test," she said. "All the time. He tries to test you. You think you have doubts? He deliberately put them in your mind so he can erase them."

A few minutes later, as she sat on the steps talking to Asha, a young man came running up to the doctor. He was out of breath and frantic, having looked everywhere for her.

"How much disinfectant should they put in the well?" he said. "They told me to ask you. Tadpoles were found in the bottom of the well."

"Two handfuls," she said without a second's hesitation, but when the young man had gone rushing back with the vital information, she laughed. "You think I know?" she said. "I don't handle that. I don't even know who does."

"But what if they put too much in or too little?"

"You think Baba would allow his own people to be poisoned by the water from his own well?"

"Then why put any disinfectant in the well at all?"

"To keep them busy, those idiots with no faith."

Later she took Asha on a tour of the ashram and as they walked past the prayer hall the doctor was stopped by Mr. Desai, the man with the son who had polio.

"My son has an earache," he told her somewhat apologetically.

She looked into the boy's ear, then reached into the cloth bag she carried and found a small bottle. Very tenderly she put a few drops of the liquid into the boy's ear.

"You'll feel better in a few minutes," she gently told the boy.

"Thank you," he said, filled almost to tears with gratitude.

As she and Asha continued on their tour Asha asked what was wrong with the boy's ear.

"I haven't the slightest idea," she said. "How could I tell without the proper instruments to look in it?"

"Then what did you put in it?"

"Mercurochrome," she said.

"Why?"

"That's all I had with me."

"You do that frequently? Just treat a person with whatever you happen to have with you?"

"I used to be cross with those fellows," she explained, "for having such little faith. But Baba told me one day I had to stop that. Be gentle, he told me, and sweet and helpful, so that's what I am, and it makes them feel better. But I could put water in his ear and if Baba willed it the deaf could hear again. He's done it hundreds of times. Did you hear about the time in, I forget just where, he called this deaf-and-dumb boy onto the stage where he was speaking one time on tour? The boy had been deaf and dumb since birth, and Baba asked him, 'What is your name?' and the boy spoke his name in front of a hundred thousand people, the first time he ever spoke in his life."

She laughed at the memory of it. "Then word got around what Baba had done and the whole street was filled the next day with deaf-and-dumb people. Poor Baba, he had to sneak out the back way to escape them."

"Why didn't he cure them?" Asha asked.

"I always used to ask him that and he would tell me to stop trying to understand him, and try to understand myself first. But it's my own opinion that everybody has his own karma and some people are ready to be cured while other people have to wait till they accumulate enough good karma before they're ready to advance to the next level so they have to suffer a little while first. But that's only my opinion."

She arranged for one of the women residents to deliver a jug full of warm water each morning to Asha and she arranged for one of the *dhobis* to pick up and deliver her laundry each day.

"Don't use that fellow," she said of one laundry man she saw soliciting business near the prayer hall. "Baba won't let him in the compound any more."

"Why not?"

"Baba used to give him his orange dresses to wash sometimes, just to help him out. But one day, Baba went for a walk in the village and he saw this long line in front of the *dhobi*'s house. He found out the fellow was charging the people two annas to see Baba's dress and four annas to touch it."

What the doctor loved to do best, though, was talk about the old days before all the people came and Baba got so busy.

"Every evening at sunset we'd go to the river, in the season when it's all dried up. Almost every night," she said, "he'd ask somebody, a different person every time, a stranger, to pick a place in the sand where we should sit so nobody would think he placed a lot of things in the sand himself or had one of his devotees do it. We'd sit there and talk, just a few of us, like a family, close and full of love. He'd start playing with the sand, pouring it from one hand to another the way a child does, and all of a sudden as the sand fell from one hand to the other you could see it turn into a ring or a necklace or a statue of Krishna. One time a great scientist was along, and Baba started teasing him about scientists believing only in what they could see instead of believing in God and the scientist said that's not true. When Dr. Oppenheimer made the first atomic bomb the first words he spoke were from the Bhagavad-Gita and Baba said to the scientist, 'You want one? Here's one for you' and he poured the sand from one hand to another and it turned into a small book of the *gita* right before our eyes. The scientist was so surprised he kept looking at the cover and the pages of the book to see if he could find anything that said where the book had been printed, and Baba laughed and said, 'My workmen don't have to print the name of their workshop.' "

"How did you first meet Baba?" Asha asked.

"In 1943, I was a student working part time in a hospital in Bangalore when this lady in the maternity ward started praying so crazy everybody came to see what she was doing. She was 'praying to Baba,' she said.

" 'Which Baba?' we asked her. Everybody is Baba. Anybody who wants to can call himself Baba.

" 'Sai Baba,' she told us.

" 'Who is Sai Baba?' we asked her.

" 'He'll be here. You'll see him,' she said.

"So when Baba arrived we were all surprised to see this boy of sixteen, so handsome, with curly hair—different than he wears it now. He had it combed down on one side over his forehead, and that sweet smile. He smiled at me and he held up both hands. That's the way he used to take things from the air in the beginning, instead of waving one hand the way he does now, and you could see whatever he made materialize in the air just over his hands and you could see it drop so gently into his hands. Well, he gave me a fig he took from the air and he told me I was going overseas in a few months to study to be a doctor. I thought he was crazy. I had no plans to be a doctor, and where could I get the money to go overseas? But six months later what he said came true, completely unexpectedly, and I didn't see him again until March 1946, when I went to some lady's house where he was supposed to visit. When he saw me he told me go to a certain temple behind my house that not too many people knew about, and meet him there the following day at a certain time. I was so surprised he knew where I lived, I asked everybody if they had told him but everybody said no. Well, I met him there and I started to see him and he would tell me everything about myself, the most intimate details. One day, I got this terrible desire to go see him at Puttaparthi and for fifteen days I tried to fight it, but finally I went. I had to go.

"As soon as I got there I went to find him. It wasn't like it is now, with so many people and everything so organized, and I found him washing his teeth at the well and I asked him could I stay there with him.

" 'Where will you stay?' he said.

" 'With your sister,' I said.

" 'What about your work?' he said. 'We have no hospital here.'

" 'I don't need a hospital,' I said. 'I need you.'

" 'No,' he said. 'I'll build one here, then you can stay with me.'

"That was in 1946 and in 1956 he did build one, the hospital, and he sent for me and I came here.

"In the old days it was different. We were just a few of us

then. Some evenings, when he wouldn't take us to the river, he'd take us to the top of the hill. One time at the hill he ran so fast up the hill we didn't even see him and then he called out to us, 'Look!' and we saw a light on his forehead so bright it hurt your eyes to look at it.

" 'My third eye,' he said.

"And he would talk and talk about everything and I didn't know what he was talking about most of the time, but he would speak with such love, such sweetness. In the old days he had time for everything, but now it's enough just to see him. That's enough, to know he's here. He has no time for any of us any more. So many people."

By the time the doctor and Asha got back to Asha's room it had already gotten dark. They stopped at the foot of the steps to listen to the young boys from Baba's school chanting Vedas in the shed across from the house. Then, suddenly, the door opened at the top of the steps and a young man about thirty, the American, stood there half in the doorway and half out. He was wearing a short-sleeved shirt over a dhoti, had long, black, curly hair and a beard which looked to be only a few weeks old. His blue eyes seemed glazed with what appeared to be either an intensity, bordering on madness, or the result of drugs.

"How the fuck can you believe in some maniac who claims he's God?" he yelled at the woman who was apparently in their room.

"You don't have to believe it," she yelled back at him.

"Don't you realize the damage he's doing? It's criminal! Criminal! Don't you realize what's going to happen to them when they find out he's nothing but a phony?"

He slammed the screen door shut and started down the steps.

"Where you going?" the woman yelled at him.

Without answering, he continued walking furiously

across the compound. The woman came to the screen door and yelled after him again. "Where you going?"

He stopped and yelled back at her, "Where the fuck you think I'm going? To steal some God-damn sugar cane!"

The woman was short and rather plump, with large breasts and waist-length, dull blond hair. She wore a dingy white sari and no shoes. After a moment Asha and the doctor could hear her crying on the porch.

"It doesn't bother us," the doctor said to Asha, "when people doubt Baba. He puts those ideas in you so he can take them away. We laugh here because we all went through that ourselves, and when we see other people going through it we know what it feels like. But you pass through that."

They sat quietly for a time, the sound of the woman crying having changed their mood, and then the doctor realized, suddenly, how exhausted Asha must be.

"Look at me babbling and you can hardly keep your eyes open," the doctor said. "Come, let me see if your room is all right."

When the doctor discovered Asha had no bedding, she wanted to try to find Surayya to see what could be found, but Asha absolutely refused to let her go to all that trouble. She finally did accept a blanket the doctor insisted upon borrowing for her from the maharaja's daughter and a small flashlight that the doctor carried in her cloth bag.

"You'll need it," the doctor said, "in case you have to get up in the middle of the night or whatever."

Finally Asha was alone in her room, and for a time she sat there on her suitcase feeling foolish and alone. She started to cry and took from her purse a small package of Kleenex, which her American friend sent her regularly along with the clippings of "Peanuts." She blew her nose and wiped her eyes, then opened her suitcase and took three Seconals, which she was able to swallow without water. She rolled up a sari to use as a pillow, stretched out on the concrete floor, and covered her head with the blanket to keep the mosquitoes from biting her face.

She knew there would be no possibility of her getting any sleep tonight, and for a time she lay there listening to the mosquitoes buzzing around her. Finally she found the courage to reach out from under the blanket and turn off the flashlight, plunging the tiny cell into syrup-thick darkness.

A few minutes later she heard a noise, a scraping sound on the wall. She reached for the flashlight, and when she turned it on she saw the small package of Kleenex moving straight up the wall. Half a second later she saw that it was being pushed up the wall by a roach at least four inches long.

Instinctively, she wheeled around and saw dozens of roaches, the same size, on the floor behind her, many having crawled into her suitcase.

She ran out to the porch.

The woman who had been crying earlier, the American, was out there, crawling into a sleeping bag.

"They're not so vicious out here," she said.

✿ EIGHT

A little before eight that night, in Whitefield, Baba was in his room upstairs waiting for Gokok and the writer. He was going over some business matters with various members of his entourage when they heard the sound of the car in the driveway. One of the men nearest the window looked out to see who it was.

"Gokok," Baba said.

It had not been at all convenient for Gokok to return to Whitefield that evening. He had to make a speech to a group at the university and, as it turned out, was nearly an hour late for his appointment with Baba.

The writer waited impatiently at Gokok's house. By the time Gokok finally arrived, the writer was barely able to be civil.

It had occurred to him that perhaps Gokok had behaved in typical Indian fashion and, in order not to hurt the writer's feelings, had told him that Baba had agreed to his writing the book when in actual fact it was perfectly possible that he had never quite gotten around to actually asking him at all.

Time after time the writer had encountered this characteristic Indian behavior, but he could never quite get used to the idea that the only motivation for lying could be sweetness, and every time it happened, it came as a surprise to him.

The most Westernized official, for example, might promise to have a car at an American's hotel precisely at a given hour, knowing full well, even as he made the promise, he had no way of providing the car, but it would have been too difficult to say that. No Indian wants to be the bearer of bad news and he will often make any kind of promise, say anything, to make the person he is dealing with happy. He is counting on the possibility that some miraculous change in circumstances will take place and that everything will turn out all right. If the miracle does not take place, of course, that only proves that it was not meant to be, and, therefore, everything has turned out for the best.

Once, at the airport in Bangalore, the writer checked in for a flight to New Delhi and the agent put his bags aside without tagging them. The writer, thinking the agent had forgotten, called it to the agent's attention.

"Oh. You want tags?" the agent said, and cheerfully found some tags in a drawer and put them on the luggage, carefully tearing off the claim checks and giving them to the writer.

"These say Calcutta," the writer said. "I'm going to New Delhi."

"Yes, yes, of course," the agent said. "It doesn't matter."

"But how do I know my bags will go to New Delhi?" the writer asked.

"Because that's where the plane is going," the agent said.

The logic was, of course, irrefutable. There was only one airplane and it was going to New Delhi, so how could the bags possibly go to Calcutta? The plane to Calcutta left on an entirely different day, but if all it would take to make the nervous American happy was a claim check, the agent was delighted to accommodate him. In addition to being for the wrong city, the writer noticed that some sound-thinking bureaucrat had seen fit to have printed on the claim check the disclaimer: "This is not a baggage check as defined by the Warsaw Convention." The writer had been given a baggage check which was not a baggage check for a city he wasn't going to—all in the interest of making him happy.

Perhaps Gokok fully intended to discuss the book with Baba, but had never quite gotten the opportunity. And finally, as the writer became more and more insistent, perhaps Gokok had written to him that Baba had agreed simply because the writer seemed to want that so much, hoping that in some way at some time before the writer actually arrived, Gokok would find the opportunity to speak to Baba about it, at which point Baba would surely agree and they would all live happily ever after.

As the chauffeur drove the writer, Gokok, and his wife who had decided at the last minute to come with them to Whitefield, the writer wanted to confront Gokok with the question directly. He realized that such a confrontation could either result in Gokok swearing that Baba had agreed to his writing the book, or, even worse, Gokok might admit that Baba had not quite agreed, not exactly, in which case all of the anger the writer had been accumulating in the weeks he waited for Baba would have been wasted, and at this point the writer needed his anger to cling to more than he needed the truth.

"What I don't understand," the writer finally said, deciding on a compromise route of attack, "is why Baba told me I could write the book and then, after I signed the contract with the publisher and went to all the expense and trouble of coming half-way around the world, why would he tell me now that I can't write it? If he didn't want me to write the book, all he had to do was say so in the beginning."

Gokok hesitated, clearly trying to find the most delicate way of saying it.

"I think he's afraid. He's indicated to me that he's a little concerned that you may not be on a high enough level spiritually."

"I didn't pretend to be on any level spiritually," the writer said.

"Yes, yes, I know," Gokok said, "but he thinks perhaps it's not possible to write about him until you have developed your spiritual self further. He told Kasturi, I think it was in 1948, that he could write a book about him, but he didn't give permission to actually do it until 1961."

"That's a little long for me to wait," the writer said. "And, anyway, if he's God, didn't he know how undeveloped I was spiritually when he agreed to let me write the book in the first place? Why should he put me through all this, leaving me like that after he promised I could go on tour with him, and now suddenly not to let me write the book at all?"

"It's very difficult to understand," Gokok said.

"I think you ought to tell him how I feel about it," the writer said, "and to point out to him that if we wait until I'm as highly evolved as Baba would like me to be, the book would come out just like Kasturi's, so full of adoration nobody in America would believe it."

"Well," Gokok ventured tentatively, "I think Baba also feels, he actually said this, that he will be very busy the next few weeks with all the people coming to Shivarathri festival. He won't have any time to give you any special attention."

"I don't want any special attention," the writer said. "All I want is to be invisible, as I said in my letters, just to watch him quietly without interfering in any way, just to be an observer."

"Yes, I'll tell him this," Gokok said.

They were silent for a time, then Gokok spoke in Telugu to his wife. The chauffeur drove as fast as he could, much too fast in the writer's view, but Gokok kept looking at his watch impatiently.

"I hate to keep him waiting," Gokok said. "They're all waiting to have dinner."

When they arrived at Whitefield they had to wait for Dixit to open the gates.

Gokok's wife had brought Dixit a jar of instant coffee for which he had to thank her, and then they had to go through the required amenities before starting up the driveway to the main house.

Before the car had completely stopped Gokok opened the door, got out, and hurried through the gate to the screened porch, his wife and the writer quickly following.

They were greeted immediately by one of the members of Baba's inner circle, a small man with a bald head and a warmingly sweet face, who hugged Gokok and bowed respectfully to Mrs. Gokok.

"Sai Ram," he said, his hands together in front of his face. Then he called to one of the young men waiting inside the reception room, asking him to tell Baba they were there. Before the young man got to the stairs, Baba came down and out to the porch.

Gokok apologized for being late, explaining that it was his fault. He had had to give a talk at the university.

"No, no," Baba said. "It's all right. It's all right."

Gokok's wife prostrated herself on the floor in front of Baba to touch his feet, but Gokok, the writer noticed, only made the respectful gesture of *Namaske*, his palms together at his chest.

Baba looked at the writer and smiled warmly, but the writer did not return the smile. He had decided there was no way Baba could win him over now.

"You didn't ask me to come," Gokok's wife said to Baba when she got up, "but I came anyway."

"You are Gokok's shadow," Baba said. "Could I ask a man to come without his shadow?"

Immediately Baba led Gokok and the writer through the reception room and into the small room used for private interviews. Gokok's wife remained on the veranda.

As soon as they sat on the floor, Gokok and the writer both facing Baba, Gokok began talking in Telugu, apparently, the writer decided, telling Baba what the writer had said in the car.

When Gokok finished, Baba turned to the writer and spoke in Telugu, with Gokok translating, phrase by phrase.

"You don't understand," Baba said. "I only told you 'Write the book' because I wanted you. Understand? You. Not a book. The book is publicity. I don't need publicity. I don't want publicity. I want you. I want your faith. I want your love. Everybody who comes here to see me thinks they have arranged it, but *I* arranged it. When the time is ready I call all of those who need me to me, when they are ready. No one can get here to see me otherwise. I want your soul, because it is time now for you to stop vacillating. You have been trying yoga, you went to Japan to study . . ." he fumbled for the word, "Zen. Buddhism. You visited several Hindu saints in India, isn't it, to find your master, but you have not found him yet. Am I right or wrong?"

For an instant the writer tried to recall whether he had ever mentioned these facts to Gokok. He did not remember having done so, but it was perfectly possible he might have, he decided, in which case Gokok could have mentioned it to Baba, placing in doubt, at least for the moment, whether Baba had demonstrated his much advertised ability to tell one "everything."

Baba looked at the writer, studying him, and then as if having read his mind spoke in almost a whisper.

"Your wife is better now," Baba said, in English.

The writer was startled.

"Before you came to India," Baba continued in Telugu, "you thought you might have to postpone the trip because a lump was discovered in her breast, but two weeks later when she went back to the doctor the lump was gone, and you wondered if I did it, but the doctor said these things often happen so you decided I didn't do it. Well, I did it. I took the lump away, which is why I am telling you this now. How else could I know of this if I didn't do it? You wondered before if you had told Gokok about studying Buddhism in Japan, but you know positively you did not mention your wife and that problem to Gokok or to anyone who knows me."

The writer knew he was expected to speak but he could only sit there, in astonishment. Then he looked up at Baba, who was watching him.

Baba smiled.

"The relationship between a master and his disciple is very special," Baba said. "You think I am treating you badly because I said, 'Go home. Don't write the book.' I am doing this for a purpose."

"What is the purpose?" the writer asked.

"That is for me to know," Baba said.

He laughed, and both Gokok and the writer laughed with him.

"Suppose a person has a thousand rupees in small coins," Baba said. "These are all of your anxieties, your problems. What I want you to do is give them to me, give them to your master and he will give you a one-thousand-rupee note. Do you understand?"

The writer nodded, but he wasn't at all sure that he did.

"I am only concerned with you and your spiritual life," Baba continued. "Not your happiness because what you call happiness is only comfort, which is why I couldn't take you on the tour. I came to your hotel room. You saw me in a dream." He laughed. "Look how he looks at Gokok to see if he mentioned that to Gokok. No, you did not mention the dream to him, did he, Gokok?"

"No," Gokok said, "I don't remember his telling me a dream."

"I came to your room," Baba said to the writer, "and saw you so unhappy and so ill and you were very unhappy because you had come here to write this book. Am I right?"

The writer nodded.

"You didn't want to go on the tour," Baba said in English, "isn't it?"

"Not completely," the writer admitted.

"So why should I take you with me?" Baba said, reverting again to Telugu. "I am so busy on these tours and there is no time to be concerned with your comfort. You are too much involved in comfort. You have your air-conditioning machines in America, and what do they give you? So when I say I am only interested in your spiritual life, I mean in your spiritual happiness, but my word for happiness, not your word. I am always in the state of happiness so that is not my concern, but I only live to give satisfaction and joy and love to my devotees. That is the only reason I live."

"If I . . ." the writer started to say.

"Forget about the book," Baba said in English, then added in Telugu: "You were about to say if you write the book you can help other people."

"Isn't it?" Baba said in English after Gokok translated.

The writer nodded.

"First is self," Baba said, "then help. Find yourself first before trying to help others. Then you can help them later."

"But I've come so far, all the way from . . ."

"Forget about far," Baba said in English. "Far is not important. No far, no near, no near. Dear, only dear is important."

Baba then began talking to Gokok in Telugu, and since Gokok didn't translate what Baba said, the writer assumed it didn't concern him. After a moment Baba turned back to the writer and said in English, "Enough about that. I am here to talk to you."

Baba looked at the writer a moment before he spoke, his fingers all the while exploring the air.

"There is a special time and a special place for each man to find his master," Baba said. "It must be the right time and the right place."

"Is this the right time and the right place for me?" the writer asked.

"You have to tell me," Baba said. "I cannot tell you."

"You have to remember," the writer said, "I come from America where everything has to be proven, but I want to be convinced and when I am, I'll be completely convinced. Until then I can only tell you it is something I want."

"Very happy," he said. "Very happy."

He placed a hand on each of the writer's shoulders, transferring an inner warmth and affection and forming a bond between them. Baba then pushed his right sleeve up over his elbow and with his fingers spread apart, his palm down, made a slow, rotating motion as he closed his fingers. When he opened them, his palm was covered with *vibhuthi*.

The writer was disappointed. He had been looking forward to receiving a gift from Baba, but he didn't want *vibhuthi*. What he had hoped to get was a picture of Baba.

Baba laughed. "Why didn't you tell me you don't want *vibhuthi*?" he said in English. "All right. I will give you what you want."

He made the same motion with his hand, and when he opened his fingers a small color photograph on aluminum, about three inches square, had materialized in his palm.

"Keep it in your pocket," Baba said, "until you have me in your heart. Then you won't need a photograph."

"Thank you," the writer said. He was very moved, but Baba had told him far too much, most of which would require a lot of time and a lot of thought, and at the moment he had taken in much more than he could assimilate.

"Come to Puttaparthi tomorrow," Baba said to the writer. "Leave your hotel about noon or one or two o'clock. I will make all the preparations for you there and when I find time I will see you as often as I can and we'll talk about the book."

NINE

Baba's caravan arrived at Puttaparthi about ten o'clock the next morning, but at least an hour before he got there the rumor had circulated that he was on his way, without anyone having received the information either by telephone or telegraph.

Baba owned five cars. Two were Fiats donated to his organization three years before, and three were Chevrolets just sent to him by a devotee from California, a Chevrolet dealer. Baba himself will accept no gifts from anyone, and he himself owns nothing, but he agreed to allow the cars to be donated to the Prasanthi Nilayam Sathya Sai Organization, one of fifteen hundred nonprofit religious corporations set up in India in Baba's name. There also are Sathya Sai organizations in Hong Kong, Singapore, Malaya, Fiji, Los Angeles, half a dozen in England, and thirty in East Africa.

Since it was incorporated as a legal township the ashram compound has been run theoretically by a township committee elected every three years by the permanent residents. Kasturi was currently chairman of the township, but they had not bothered to elect any other officers specifically, although seven people, including Dr. Jayalakshmi and Surayya, were on the council. No decision, however inconsequential, was made by anyone other than Baba. All of the housing units were paid for individually by the various devotees who built them after having gotten Baba's permission to do so, and the construction of the prayer hall and hospital was paid for by donations to the Sathya Sai Organization.

About five hundred men and women lived permanently at the ashram, including about one hundred women. All these were widows and they lived in one large shed without partitions exactly like the sheds built for visitors except for the fact that the women's dormitory had walls.

As soon as Baba's cars appeared in the distance, about five minutes away, most of the people at the ashram rushed to the main gate to see him and followed the cars when they drove inside the compound until they stopped near the prayer hall.

When Baba got out of the car he was greeted by Kasturi and Surayya, and after briefly acknowledging the presence of those who had come to see him, Baba and the members of his inner circle went upstairs to his living quarters over the prayer hall.

Mr. Desai, who had been to the ashram before, did not carry his son to see Baba get out of the car, but instead took the opportunity to get the best place to sit outside of the prayer hall, directly in front of the door Baba would come out of to select people for private interviews.

The merchant from Ceylon had rushed to his room to tell his wife that Baba was coming, but by the time they got there the crowd was so large around the cars neither he nor his wife could catch a glimpse of Baba.

Steve and Eloise, the American couple, had joined the crowd, but when Eloise pushed her way through so that she could see Baba, Steve would not go along with her, choosing instead to stay apart from the crowd and aloof from them.

The doctor and the maharaja's daughter stood together on a small hill above the crowd. When they finally saw Baba get out of the car, neither could quite suppress her joy. They waited until Baba disappeared around the other side of the prayer hall, then the young girl went back to her room and the doctor went down the hill to the group around the prayer hall, where she saw Steve and went to him.

"Maybe you'll see him today," she said. "He usually gives private interviews to all the foreigners between ten and eleven o'clock every day. But sometimes, on the first day, he has so many matters to attend to he can't find the time, but if not today, tomorrow then or the next day."

"Yeah," Steve said. "Sure. That's fine."

The doctor hurried around to the other side of the prayer hall, hoping to catch a glimpse of Baba should he decide to come out on the balcony. Eloise, who had followed the crowd around the prayer hall, came back to Steve.

"Did you see him?" she asked.

"No," he said.

He turned and started walking across the compound toward their room. She followed him.

"Where you going?" she said.

"To turn on," he said, then he stopped. "You know what? Let's drop some acid before the interview. Wouldn't that blow your mind, to meet God on acid?"

Steve had been a merchant seaman until the ship's captain had him arrested for possessing pornographic photographs, a charge which could have been made against most of the sailors on the ship, he claimed. Everybody on the ship hated him, he said, because of his politics and they just used that "to get rid of me."

The jail sentence kept him out of the draft, and for over a

year he had been hitchhiking wherever the impulse took him. He had no plans for the future. He didn't want to be anything or do anything except perhaps accumulate knowledge, as long as it was for no particular purpose or related to any particular subject.

"He'll be all right," the doctor told the writer one evening, after Steve had behaved with his usual hostility. "Even with your Christian saints, the ones who started out so crazy always turned out to be the ones who did the most."

Eloise was not married to Steve. She had a husband who abandoned her in California with a two-year-old baby. She later left the baby with her mother so she could hitchhike to India. She met Steve on the road from Benares to Calcutta and they had been together for nearly six months.

They were in Madras when they heard about Baba and they thought they might as well hitchhike down to see him, just for the hell of it. As they were walking through town, they were stopped by an Indian man who asked them if they'd like to make a few rupees as extras in a movie.

"Sure," they said, and they went with the man to the movie studio where they, along with a number of other Americans, were supposed to be members of an audience in a theater watching some kind of show. Nobody ever told them what kind of show, all the director kept yelling was "React! React!"

After it was over the man who recruited them paid them and Steve noticed it was less than the amount he had been promised.

"I took out twenty-five per cent for my commission," the man explained. "As the agent."

"You just hold on a minute, buddy," Steve said. "If you told us that up front, okay. But you can't come around with that shit now."

"That's the way we do it in India," the man said.

"Well, here's the way we do it in America," Steve said, grabbing the man's fountain pen from his pocket and breaking it in two over his knee.

"Listen," the man said, getting frightened, "if you want the money I'll give you the money out of my own pocket."

"I consider myself paid," Steve said, shoving the two halves of the fountain pen into the man's pocket.

With the money they got for being extras Steve and Eloise took the bus to Puttaparthi, where Surayya automatically housed them in one of the rooms saved for Americans.

In the two weeks they had been waiting for Baba, Eloise had completely submerged herself in the ashram routine, attending every *bhajan* session, helping the women each day in the water brigade, starting a notebook of useful Telugu phrases, and a cookbook of local recipes. In direct proportion to her adjustment to the place, Steve had become more and more hostile—to Baba, to the ashram, and especially to Eloise.

Quietly she began inquiring what the possibilities would be for her to stay at the ashram, asking the doctor if they would let her stay there permanently if she went back to America to get her child and returned.

"Only Baba can give you that answer," the doctor said. What had started out as a vague idea in Eloise's mind gradually grew into a desperate hope and finally into a concrete plan that she had come to accept as the only possible solution to her life.

Meanwhile, as the days passed, Steve spent his time thinking up new and more diabolic ways to expose Baba and embarrass him when they got to see him.

"I'll show that fucking phony up for what he really is," Steve kept saying to anyone who would listen.

His threats only amused the doctor. "He isn't the first

person we ever saw who wanted to ruin Baba," she said. "Baba put all that hostility in the boy so he can take it away. You'll see, it always happens, the minute he sees Baba he'll turn into a baby kitten."

Asha was walking through the village when she saw the commotion through the ashram gates, but by the time she got to the prayer hall Baba had already gone. She stood for a moment, not knowing what to do or where to go and then, seeing everyone finding places to sit in front of the prayer hall, she sat down in the dirt, too. Almost immediately a very stiff, very stern white-haired woman in her sixties, wearing an orange sari, came up to Asha and started shouting at her in Telugu.

"I don't understand," Asha said in Hindi. "Do you speak Hindi?"

The woman, however, only repeated the same thing but louder, and had just grabbed Asha's arm when the doctor came along and quieted the old woman, in Telugu, telling her she would take care of the situation. The woman shouted at Asha once more, for good measure, then turned and looked for someone else to shout at, roughly pushing a young boy out of the way as she went.

"The women sit over there," the doctor told Asha gently. "Come, I'll show you where to sit so he'll see you."

Asha got up and went with the doctor to the other end of the prayer hall, where a number of women already were seated on the ground.

"What am I supposed to do?" Asha asked.

"Usually," the doctor said, "he comes out about eleven o'clock, at *bhajan* time, and he'll pick about fifty people for interviews, but today, I don't know. Would you like me to speak to Kasturi and tell him you've come a long way? Maybe he could see you special."

"No," Asha said. "I'll wait here."

Asha sat in the dirt near the woman with two children. The doctor looked around a moment. Then she started back toward the hospital.

On the other side of the prayer hall she saw a young Indian man trying to take a snapshot of Baba's mother, who was sitting in the dirt in front of her room, number eighty-six, which was in a building containing seven other rooms directly behind the prayer hall. The old woman was senile, and spent most of her time sitting in front of her house until the sun reached the point where the building no longer offered any shade, at which time she would go into the house and grind rice with a stone or, when it was time, cook her own meals.

"Get away from me," the old woman yelled in Telugu. "Don't point that thing at me. Get away from me!"

The young man, embarrassed, prostrated himself in front of her, wanting to touch her feet, but she slapped his hand away.

"Get away from me," she yelled.

The doctor went to them and shouted at Baba's mother, treating her as if she were a naughty child. "Stop that," she said. "Stop acting so silly." Then she turned to the young man. "Take all the pictures you want."

Baba's mother obediently held still for two pictures, then she started yelling at the young man again. The doctor shouted at the old woman to behave herself.

"That's fine," the man said to the doctor. He turned to Baba's mother and touched her feet. "Thank you. Thank you very much. Thank you."

As the young man hurried away, Baba's mother started complaining to no one in particular: "Why don't they leave him alone? Look how they make him work. He doesn't sleep, he doesn't eat enough. All they care about is themselves. They want to kill him. He doesn't eat because he doesn't like their cooking. He likes my cooking." And then she looked at the doctor. "Doesn't he like my cooking any more?"

"Very much," the doctor said.

✤ TEN

That day in November 1926, when Baba's mother started having labor pains, it was sunrise. She, along with many other people in the village, was chanting the names of Siva. It was a holy day, a Monday of the holy month of Karthika, made even more auspicious because the ascendant star was Ardra and on such rare occasions when the month, the day, and the star coincide special pujas are required. Easwaramma, which is the name of Baba's mother, had just finished her Sathyanarayana puja when she started having intense contractions. She went home and sent word to her mother-in-law, who was the head of the household, that she was about to give birth, but the mother-in-law was in the middle of her prayers at the house of the priest and refused either to interrupt them or be hurried. When she returned home, in her own good time, she brought the flowers and the sacred water from the ceremony to bless the grandson she knew would be born. He was named Sathyanarayana in honor of the puja.

In the biography written by Kasturi it is said that when the baby was placed on a blanket immediately after birth the midwife noticed something moving under the blanket. When she looked under it she and the other women in the room saw a cobra, which throughout India is regarded as the symbol of royalty. A child found with a cobra guarding it with outspread hood or a child born with a birthmark resembling the hood was, in ancient India, immediately given royal status.

One of Baba's two sisters, however, who claims to have been present at his birth, says that the cobra was not found under the blanket, but several hours after Baba was born a cobra was seen outside the house, a sight not uncommon in the village.

For every story about Baba's childhood there are any number of conflicting stories and, at this point, the writer discovered, it is no longer possible to sift out the facts from the legend. For one thing Baba has forbidden his family and devotees to talk about his childhood and "they all live in terror of Baba," as one of his most devoted followers told the writer. "When they do something wrong," the devotee said, "he won't look at them or speak to them for days and it's agony for them. He is their whole life and if he rejects them or tells them to leave they have nothing left. If you do something wrong Baba will tell you about it three times. The first time he will tell you in private to stop doing it. The second time, if you still keep doing it, he will tell you about it in front of everybody in the prayer hall, like: 'I have told you to stop doing such and such a thing and yet you continue doing it.' Everybody is very afraid of his doing this to them—because the next time, if you still keep doing it, he just tells you to leave and you can beg him all you like but it won't do you any good. When he tells you to leave you have to leave, and where does a person go when God tells you to leave? Whom do you turn to?"

There is a story about Raj Reddy, the son of the maharaja, who gave up everything to drive Baba's car and look after his personal needs. Once, according to the story, he got permission from Baba to go home and visit his family but with instructions to return on a specific day in time for a particular festival. The day before the prince was supposed to leave and return to Puttaparthi his grandmother died and his family convinced him that he should stay an extra day or two. When he got back to the ashram, two days late, Baba would not talk to him. When Raj would bring Baba his pan, Baba would turn away as if he did not see Raj. This went on for five days until the prince broke down and, crying, begged Baba to forgive him. He couldn't stand it any longer. He couldn't sleep. He couldn't eat. Finally, Baba said to him, "Why do you think I have these festivals to celebrate my birthday and things like that? For me? I don't need that. For you. My people. And when it comes time for you to choose, who did you pick, me or a corpse?"

At first the writer was suspicious about the reason why Baba had imposed such severe restrictions against his followers relating stories about his childhood, but he later came to believe that it wasn't Baba's intention to suppress information he was afraid might be revealed. Instead, the writer decided, it was the simplest way to keep Baba's well-meaning devotees from distorting the truth. A slight exaggeration here, an embellishment there could ultimately contaminate his entire reservoir of credibility.

It was not possible to document with certifiable evidence very much of Baba's biography. But with the help of Kasturi, who contacted many people who had figured importantly in Baba's life and convinced them it would be all right to speak about it, the writer gradually was able to piece together some kind of picture of Baba's childhood and rise to eminence.

In some cases interpreters were needed to interpret the

interpreters, as in the case of the interviews with one of Baba's sisters who spoke only Telugu. At that particular time the available interpreters were a young man who spoke only Hindi and English, but no Telugu, and another young man who spoke Telugu and Hindi but no English. Everything the sister said had to be translated by one of the young men from Telugu into Hindi and then by the other young man from Hindi into English. Not only was this procedure frustratingly time-consuming but after being filtered through two separate and distinct personalities, what the writer was told the sister said might very well have been something quite different from what she actually said.

Baba was born a Brahmin in Puttaparthi on November 23, 1926, in a house that now exists only as ruins, having long ago been washed away by the floods. His ancestors were responsible for building the temple in honor of the stone that killed the snake, and, about fifty yards away, Baba's grandfather built another temple in honor of Radha, the young and beautiful mortal Lord Krishna fell in love with.

The grandfather, Sri Ratnakara Kondama Raju, lived until 1950, when he died at the age of a hundred and ten. His wife died about twenty years before he did, and in violation of the Hindu custom the old man wouldn't live with his sons as he was supposed to. He chose instead a separate cottage which made him something of an iconoclast in the village. The need for privacy is not something Indians either approve of or understand.

When his son, Pedda (Baba's father) married Easwaramma, a distant cousin, they quickly had one son and two daughters, but they longed for another son so Easwaramma prayed to all the village gods. She took a number of sacred vows, endured long periods of fasting and other acts of sacrifice, but not until years later, when her children were al-

ready married, did she finally become pregnant again with
the son who later would be called Baba but was called
Sathya as a child.

In trying to discover what Sathya's childhood was like the
writer ran across every possible variation from "he was an
ordinary child, like the rest of us" to stories of precocious
saintliness which told of how, when he was only five years
old, he frequently went without food so that he could sneak
it out of the house and give it to the beggars and blind men
in the village.

It is generally accepted that at the age of seven he started
writing religious songs which were performed at the village
festivals. When he was eight he was allowed to advance to
the higher elementary school, which was in a village about
two and a half miles from where he lived. Every morning,
after a breakfast of cold rice and curds, or cooked raggee
rice and chutney (food he still eats), he would have to walk,
as the other children did, through the fields, which in the
rainy season were often flooded neck deep.

He was about eight or nine years old when he first began
materializing objects out of the air, usually candy, according
to his former classmates (most of whom still live in Puttaparthi and are not, for the most part, devotees). He would
take an empty bag, they recalled, and would keep pulling
candy out of it until all of his friends had their fill. When
they asked him how he did it, he said a certain village saint,
whom they had never heard of, obeyed his will and would
give him whatever he wanted.

Baba's sister still cherishes and proudly displays a shriv-
eled lime which she claims was the first object she ever saw
him materialize. She was in a hospital in Bangalore at the
time and Baba, about thirteen or fourteen, came to see her.
He said he would give her something to make her well. He
then held both hands above his head as if about to catch a

ball. A second later the lime appeared above him, hung in mid-air for an instant, then dropped gently into his hands.

His sister was so amazed, she refused to drink the juice from it. She wanted to keep it. So he produced another one in exactly the same way, telling her she could keep the first one if she drank the juice from the second one.

With the exception of the grandfather, the rest of the Raju family lived together in one house as was, and still is, the custom, and Baba grew up in a family of eighteen cousins. He took part in all of the musical plays and festivals held in the village, and when he was ten formed a *bhajan* group.

When Sathya's older brother got a job as a teacher of Telugu at the only high school in the area, in Uravakonda, a village not too far away, it was decided that as Sathya was being groomed for a college education so that he might become a civil service officer, he should go to live with his brother in order to attend the high school.

One evening, when Sathya was fourteen and living with his brother, he suddenly screamed and, holding his right toe, fell to the ground.

It was assumed he had been bitten by a scorpion but a search by those who were with him could not reveal one. To his brother's relief Sathya slept well that night, without any sign of pain. But by the end of the next day he was stiff and .unconscious, and could breathe only with great difficulty.

A doctor was called and the next morning Sathya seemed to be out of danger.

For several days, though, Sathya's behavior seemed odd. He would not eat and for long periods he wouldn't speak and then suddenly, he'd start screaming as loudly as he could or start singing religious songs no one had ever heard before. Or he would babble what seemed like gibberish or begin a discussion of Vedanta which was on such a high level, philosophically, that neither his brother nor any of the neighbors could understand what he was saying.

A letter was immediately sent to Baba's parents, telling them to come as quickly as they could; but due to a number of complications it took his parents about a week to arrive at Uravakonda. His brother recalls that on the day the parents finally arrived he had become so anxious about what might have happened to them along the way that he arranged for a man to start toward Puttaparthi on a bicycle and see if he could find the parents stranded somewhere. While the brother was giving the man directions about how to get there, Sathya interrupted and said it would not be necessary for the man to go because his parents would arrive in half an hour. Exactly half an hour later, the brother remembers, they arrived.

When the parents saw the way the boy was behaving they didn't know what to make of it. Frequently, he would grow stiff and appear to leave his body. This was something every Indian is familiar with, either having seen a yogi perform it or heard about it. It had never occurred to either his parents or his brother or his brother's wife that Sathya could possibly have become holy in some way. His peculiar behavior only confused them.

One day, Sathya complained that a neighbor who was considered a leading scholar in the community had been interpreting one of the Vedas all wrong and demanded that they bring the scholar to him so that he might correct the man.

The scholar was annoyed to have this boy insult him and at first refused to even consider meeting with the boy. Finally, when it began to look in the eyes of the community as if the scholar might be afraid of a confrontation, he consented to go to Sathya's house. The boy began cross-examining him, pointing out section after section where the old man misinterpreted the text. According to the story, the old scholar was so impressed he fell at the boy's feet and begged his forgiveness for not coming to him immediately.

Meanwhile, the medical officer from Anantapur, which is the district headquarters, happened to be camping in the village at the time so the doctor who was treating Sathya went to him for help.

After examining the boy the medical officer said that Sathya was suffering from hysteria. It had nothing to do with the scorpion bite the boy might or might not have received. He prescribed some medication, which was followed for three days, but the symptoms became worse. For long periods Sathya would alternately laugh hysterically or cry uncontrollably. Occasionally he would claim to have visited places which no one had ever heard of, giving minute details of what he saw there.

Astrologers were called in and after ample consultations and computations their conclusion was that the boy had been possessed by a ghost who, they decided, had been the first tenant of the house in which Sathya's brother lived. They scolded the brother for not being more careful in the selection of a house and left. Magicians were called in and they diagnosed the strange behavior as being due to a sudden traumatic experience which terrified the boy and upset the wave lengths of his nervous system. A number of priests were asked for their advice and they recommended the family give generously to the temple.

Finally, it was decided that the spirit of the boy had indeed been occupied by a ghost and an exorciser was found and brought to see the boy. Sathya quickly got rid of him by berating him fiercely for having the audacity to come there under the pretext of trying to cure the very person he had been worshiping every day of his life. The man's business was to continue worshiping him, the boy said, ap-

parently in such a convincing tone that the man left immediately, without even trying to collect the fee which he and
the boy's parents had agreed upon. When the boy's father
went to the man to ask why he wouldn't help Sathya, the
man said he could not help him because the boy was positively in touch with God and not in any way connected
with the Devil.

Discouraged and no longer having any place in the village
to turn, the parents took Sathya back to Puttaparthi and
there the boy's behavior became even more bizarre.

In Puttaparthi other men were brought in to exorcise the
ghost, which the parents now fully believed was the result
of some enemy's black magic, but Sathya only laughed at
these men and in time each of them gave up.

One day, the parents were given the name of a famous
exorciser who, they were told, was the most accomplished
in all India. He was a believer in Shakti (Siva's wife, who,
like her husband, is worshiped as the destroyer as well as
the creator and is usually personified as a cruel, ugly mon-
ster with blood dripping from her mouth). Sathya's parents
took the boy on the long journey by bullock cart to
the village where the exorciser lived. On the way they endured breakdowns, fever, and diarrhea until at last they
reached the home of this famous man who, it is said, was
gigantic, with blood-red eyes and a terrifyingly wild
manner of behavior.

He looked at the boy for a time in silence. Sathya laughed.
The parents watched them, waiting eagerly, hopefully.

After a long period of time, the man said he could with
absolute certainty chase the Devil out of the boy's spirit. He
began by sacrificing a chicken. When this had no effect, he
killed a lamb, after which he made the boy sit in the center
of a circle of blood while he chanted a number of magic
words. There were no noticeable signs of improvement.

Ordinarily, the exorciser said, this would have chased out a normal ghost but this ghost must indeed be the Devil himself, so he insisted the parents allow him to progress to a more advanced technique.

The parents agreed. As they watched, the exorciser shaved the boy's head and, with a knife, made three crosses which covered the boy's scalp from the back of his head to his forehead. Sathya endured the pain silently. Then while the scalp was open and bleeding the exorciser poured lime juice, garlic, and acids into the open wound. The parents begged the man to stop, but the boy neither cried nor protested.

When this treatment failed to get rid of the ghost, the exorciser suggested another treatment. Reluctantly the parents agreed. Every day for almost a week a hundred and eight pots of cold water were poured onto the scalp wound. This didn't exorcise the ghost either. The man began another treatment. He started beating the boy ritualistically with a heavy stick to drive out what he called "stag fever" when the boy walked, and "rock fever" when he was still.

When this failed, too, the man said he had one treatment left and even the Devil could not withstand this one. It was called the *kalikam*. As the parents watched he concocted a mixture of various kinds of acids and herbs which was then applied to the boy's eyes. Very quickly Sathya's entire head and face swelled up. His eyes became red and tears poured from them. His entire body shivered with pain.

The man was pleased. It would only be a short time now, he assured the parents, and then the boy would be cured.

Sathya's father is now dead but Kasturi, who reports on this incident, related that the father and the mother (who at the time Kasturi got the story from her was not yet senile) both said that through all of this pain Sathya never once made a sound.

As Sathya lay shivering with obvious agony the exorciser had to leave the room to prepare another application. He told the parents that under no circumstances should they go near their son or try to console him.

When he left the room, however, the mother could not bear watching her son in such terrible agony. She went to Sathya to touch him and comfort him. When she bent down to the boy he whispered to her, and told her to prepare a specific combination of ingredients and meet him at a certain place some distance from the house in an hour.

The mother was torn between wanting to help her son by giving him immediate comfort and wanting to help him by getting the ghost exorcised. At last, she could no longer stand to see him suffering and went to gather together the ingredients he asked her to get.

The man came back into the room and applied another concoction to Sathya's eyes and face, then left the room. The boy got up. He was barely able to move, but somehow he managed to make his way to the place where he was to meet his mother. She was there when he got there and he mixed the various herbs together which she had brought to him and applied them to his eyes, which were now almost completely closed. Within minutes after he applied the ointment the swelling went down, his mother later told Kasturi.

When the exorciser discovered what had happened he was furious.

"I was within an inch of saving that boy," he shouted.

Sathya's father paid the man his entire fee, and, out of guilt, gave him several gifts in addition. Then they began their long trip back to Puttaparthi.

When they returned home the boy's behavior seemed to be even more peculiar than it had been previously and whenever the parents heard of someone who might be able to help, they immediately sought his opinion.

On Thursday, May 23, Sathya got up as usual and for the first time in months he seemed happy. He called the entire family around him and started materializing candy and flowers, which he gave to each of them. When the neighbors heard what was happening, many came into the house to see for themselves and he gave them flowers and candy, too. To some he gave bowls of rice.

Sathya's father was working some distance away from the house at the time and when someone came to tell him what was happening he left his work and came rushing home, having to force his way through the crowd to get into the room where the boy was holding court.

"What are you people doing here?" the father asked the neighbors.

They told him of the miracles the boy had been performing, and one of them had the audacity to tell the father to go and wash his feet and hands before approaching the boy. This infuriated the father, who thought his son was merely doing some kind of cheap magician's tricks, and, having had enough nonsense from the boy, he picked up a stick, threatened to hit his son with it, and yelled at him: "What are you doing? Are you supposed to be a saint or a ghost or just plain crazy? Tell me!"

"I am Sai Baba," the boy said.

No one had ever heard the name Sai Baba.

"What do you mean?" the father asked.

"Venkavadhootha prayed that I would be born in your family so I came."

They didn't know who Venkavadhootha was either. (Much later, they discovered that according to a family legend there had been a great ancestral sage by that name who was considered a guru by thousands of people in the surrounding villages until his death in Mysore State.)

The father knew the word *sai* was Persian and was afraid

that Sai Baba was actually a Moslem speaking through the
boy so he asked him, "What are we supposed to do?"

"Worship me," the boy said.

"When?"

"Every Thursday."

Word quickly spread throughout the village and eventually it was discovered that a government official who had
visited a nearby village some time ago was a devotee of a
fakir who called himself Sai Baba. The holy man lived in
Shirdi, a village nearly two thousand miles from Puttaparthi.
Since the parents did not see how their son could possibly
have heard about him, unless indeed his spirit were truly
haunted by the ghost of this saint, it was decided the boy
should be taken to see this government worker in the hope
that perhaps he might be able to help them understand what
was going on.

After considerable difficulty, the government worker was
found. Against his better judgment, he agreed to speak to
the boy. After a short conversation the man said the boy
was suffering from a clear case of mental derangement and
his parents were advised to get him to an institution as soon
as possible.

"Yes, it is a mental derangement," Baba is said to have
replied. "But whose? You can't seem to recognize the very
Sai whom you say you worship."

The boy then materialized handfuls of *vibhuthi* and scattered them all about the room.

When they returned to Puttaparthi and the neighbors
were told what had taken place one of them said to Sathya,
"If you are Sai Baba, then show us some proof."

"Give me those jasmine flowers," Sathya said, and after
receiving them he threw the flowers to the floor.

The flowers, according to those present, fell so that they
formed the Telugu words for Sai and Baba.

Nevertheless, Sathya was again sent to live with his brother and continue his schooling. But by now he had achieved a kind of notoriety and while many considered him either mad or an impostor, others came to him each Thursday to offer flowers and sweets and to get his blessing. Occasionally he would offer them *vibhuthi* which he materialized, and on one or two occasions he is said to have materialized pictures of Shirdi.

One day, a number of teachers from the high school came to expose the boy. If he were in some way holy, as he claimed, he should have no trouble answering the questions they proposed to ask him. And so, for several hours they cross-examined him on Vedanta and philosophical matters. To their amazement he not only answered all of their questions but asked them questions they could not answer and then proceeded to tell them what the answers were. He also asked them to ask him questions, all speaking at the same time. After a few minutes of babble, which none of the witnesses present could understand, the boy proceeded to answer each question that had been shouted at him, taking each teacher, one by one, in turn.

On one Thursday Sathya is said to have cured a chronic tuberculosis patient with *vibhuthi* he materialized, and to demonstrate the fact that he had been cured, he had the man walk a mile.

On October 20, 1940, Sathya made the final break with his family and his past life. He started for school that morning as usual, accompanied by the excise inspector, Sri Anjaneyuhi, who had grown very fond of the boy. When they got to the schoolyard Sathya stopped, and, as reported later by the excise inspector, a very bright halo appeared around Sathya's face. He turned without a word and started back toward his house. When he got there he threw his books down outside the door and called to his sister-in-law inside.

"I am no longer your Sathya," he shouted. "I am Sai."

His sister-in-law came out of the house and she too was almost blinded by the halo around his head. She closed her eyes and screamed.

"I am going," the boy said. "I don't belong to you. My students are calling me. I have my work, I cannot stay here any longer."

The boy's brother was quickly called and a neighbor, Sri Narayana Sastri, hearing the noise, came running. He, too, saw the halo and fell at the boy's feet.

"Give up trying to cure me," Sathya told his brother when he came. "I am Sai. I do not consider myself related to you."

The brother pleaded for Sathya to stay at least until his parents could be sent for, but the boy would not step into the house again. He moved into the garden near the house of the excise inspector and sat there on a rock as dozens of people started coming to pay homage to him. Sathya led them in the singing of *bhajans* and he taught them a new one he composed: "Meditate in thy mind on the feet of the guru. They alone can take you across the difficult sea of *Samsara* (the world of births and deaths)."

The boy stayed in the garden three days. One evening, while he was singing with the group that had gathered around him, he stopped and seemed to listen a moment.

"*Maya* (illusion) has come," he said.

At precisely this moment, Sathya's mother arrived from Puttaparthi. The boy left the group and went to his brother's house, where his mother began to cry and plead with him to come home and pray to her own God for help.

"But who belongs to whom?" Sathya said. "Everything is *Maya*."

A few days later Sathya went back with his mother to Puttaparthi. When they left, a group of devotees, organized by the excise inspector, formed a procession led by musicians to escort the boy to the boundaries of the next village.

Baba lived a short while with his parents in Puttaparthi, then he moved to the house of his mother's brother. By this time the wife of the *karnam* (the village chief) had become an avid follower of the boy, and she invited Baba to move in with her family. The *karnam*, whose office is handed down from generation to generation, rules the village almost single-handedly, and, by sponsoring Sathya, made his holiness much easier to accept among those who had doubted it.

After a time the *karnam*'s wife, Subbamma, was devoting her entire time to Sathya, who was now called Baba. She cooked his meals, washed his clothes, and welcomed the growing numbers of people who came to see him.

Soon so many people were coming, many out of curiosity, that Baba felt he could not make them wait until Thursday and he began to conduct services every day. He would speak of God, lead the group in singing *bhajans*, and occasionally produce *vibhuthi* and other gifts for his followers.

When his room became too small to accommodate the large number of people who came each day to see him, the *karnam*'s wife had a shed built near their house. Repeatedly the shed had to be enlarged as pilgrims from all of the villages in the area began arriving to stay for days or weeks.

The next year, as Baba's reputation spread, a famous swami, Digambara, came to Puttaparthi to expose the boy. The swami had meditated for so many years without moving that he had lost the use of both of his legs. He had also renounced clothing and had taken a vow of total silence. Any one of these accomplishments would have been enough to establish him as a great sage, but having all three endowed the old man with an aura of sainthood.

As he was carried, naked, into the village, word was quickly spread about the impending confrontation. Holy man against holy man is a sport as popular in India as bull-fighting is in Madrid.

The old sage was carried through the village and placed on the ground in front of the *karnam*'s house.

The huge crowd which had gathered around him waited to see what Baba would do. Presently the boy came out. For a moment he just looked at the old man. The old man glared at him. Neither the boy nor the old man flinched. Then Baba spoke.

"If you have cut off all relationship with society," the boy said, "as your nakedness indicates, then why don't you go to a cave in the forest away from people?"

Suddenly Baba materialized a towel, which he offered the old man.

"Put this on," Baba said.

The old man did not take the towel.

"I know," Baba said, gently. "You are afraid you may not get food if you go to the forest, but you will, I promise you. I shall see to that. Everywhere you go I shall give you food regularly, but don't wander about naked and give all this bother to these good people who carry you about from place to place."

According to several people who claim to have witnessed the incident, the old man began to cry, and then he took the towel from Baba's hand and touched Baba's feet.

When word of Baba's victory spread, more people started coming to see him, including many devotees of Shirdi who came to see for themselves if their master had really returned.

Many found fault with Baba for spending so much of his time on physical and mental illnesses instead of spiritual work, but his answer was that in order to reach people spiritually it was first necessary to cure their pain.

Many holy men still complain about the fact that Baba indulges himself with cheap tricks of materialization, not that they doubt his ability to materialize physical objects, many yogis can materialize and dematerialize concrete objects, but those kinds of feats are considered to be on the lowest level, spiritually. A true saint should live in a cave, away from society, without cheapening himself by becoming popular, they insist.

"My miracles," Baba has said, "are my calling cards. I give the people what they want so that they will later give me what I want, their love of God. Some people may call it advertising, and, if it is, so be it. I am here to serve my devotees the best way I can."

As Baba's reputation spread people in surrounding villages and cities wanted to see him, but they had no way of getting to Puttaparthi so Baba began making tours of the area.

It was in Bangalore that Baba performed his first operation, materializing all of the instruments necessary to cut out a duodenal ulcer.

Not everyone believed in him, however, and many people in the village, which had by this time gone almost completely communist, openly tried to degrade and humiliate him. Once during a festival someone tried to poison him.

Baba and two of his devotees were visiting a number of houses in Puttaparthi, and in each house, according to custom, he and the members of his party were given food that courtesy compelled them to eat. At one house he looked at the food and, without explanation, refused to allow the members of his party to eat what had been offered them—adding to their confusion by eating both of their portions as well as his own. When he left the house, he told his two companions that the food had been poisoned. Then he laughed and vomited the food he had just eaten. One of the men who was with him claims he secretly took some of the food and tested it to see if it was poisoned or not, giving it to one of the many hungry dogs. The dog died.

By 1945 so many people were coming to see Baba it became impossible for him to continue living at the home of the *karnam*. It is also intimated, although no one is willing to be quoted, that a great deal of conflict was beginning to build up between the *karnam* and Baba.

Several of Baba's devotees wanted to build him a temple of his own. They asked Baba for permission to buy a piece of land near the temple of the rock that killed the snake, and eventually he authorized them to build a simple stone house for him there.

Part of the building was used exclusively as a prayer hall, while Baba lived in a small adjoining room.

The *karnam*'s wife continued to serve as his loyal disciple, personally tending to the hundreds of people who were now arriving every day. She ground the rice and coconuts, and cooked the food to feed them. This left very little time for her to devote to her family which, it is said, further incensed the *karnam*.

Every evening Baba and his followers staged a procession along the dusty bullock trail that winds through the village. Baba, on a palanquin, would be carried on the shoulders of those lucky devotees he would select each day for this honor. During the procession he plucked flowers from the garlands which had been placed around his neck, and tossed the petals to the people he passed. Often when the petals reached the hands of the people who caught them, they were no longer petals, but had become medallions with Baba's picture on one side and Shirdi's on the other, or sometimes pieces of candy.

Frequently during the processions young men would throw rocks or vegetables or manure at Baba, but these people, Baba's devotees claim, were merely carrying out the *karnam*'s orders.

Even before Baba's small temple had been completed it had become too small for the large number of people who came to see him, so a corrugated tin roof was put up in front of the temple. Even that became too small, and before the year was over a separate house had been built for Baba to live in behind the temple.

By 1948 Baba's devotees had become convinced that it no longer would be possible for him to live in the midst of all that noise and dirt and confusion. On festival days the area became intolerably chaotic, they felt, and they asked Baba to give them permission to raise enough money to build an ashram large enough to accommodate his following, which was multiplying every day.

Many people (none of whom would consent to be quoted) told the writer that one of the important motivating factors in Baba's decision to build an ashram was that he already had acquired the necessary backing of high-ranking government officials to have the ashram incorporated as a separate township, thereby escaping the *karnam*, who, it is said, kept asking for higher and higher taxes.

Toward the end of the year Baba gave his devotees permission to raise the money to buy the land and start construction on the compound, which he said would be named Prasanthi Nilayam.

The prayer hall was the first building to be constructed, with Baba's living quarters on the floor above. Baba designed every detail himself. But when he told the men in charge of construction what he wanted, they said it would be impossible. How, for example, could they possibly bring heavy steel girders from the nearest train station, sixteen miles away? There was no road and, in addition, they would have to be carried across the sand of the dried-up river. Even if they could somehow cross the river, how could they possibly hoist such heavy steel beams without machinery?

"Don't worry," Baba said. "I'll take care of it."

One night, while the chief engineer was asleep, he was awakened by a loud noise in front of his house. He looked out, and to his surprise saw a crane. When he went outside to investigate, he discovered that the crane was on its way to a dam which was being constructed nearby, but the crane had broken down in front of the engineer's house and the driver could not make it move.

The engineer went to see the man in charge of the operation.

"If I can repair it," the engineer said, "will you let me use it first, before taking it to the dam?"

The man in charge had nothing to lose. It would take weeks to get someone from central headquarters in Bangalore to come out and fix the crane, so he agreed. The engineer immediately went to Puttaparthi to tell Baba what had happened.

Before the engineer could say a word, Baba told him what had happened and materialized a handful of *vibhuthi*, which he gave to the engineer, telling him to scatter it over the crane's motor and it would start.

The engineer returned to the crane in front of his house and followed Baba's instructions. Immediately the engine started.

The engineer took the crane to the railroad station and started hauling the heavy steel girders toward Puttaparthi, but again the crane broke down at the banks of the dried-up river.

This time when the engineer went to Baba he said that with all due respect to his miraculous powers, it did not seem possible to cross the hundred yards of sand with such a heavy load, even if the motor were made to start again. Baba went to the river himself, and without ever having seen a crane before, got into the cab and drove it across the sand, then over the rocky trail to the place where the temple was to be constructed.

On November 23, 1950, Baba's twenty-fourth birthday, the temple at Prasanthi Nilayam was officially inaugurated.

☙ELEVEN

Until Baba arrived at the ashram the writer had never seen a policeman there, although he had been told four were on duty. Minutes after Baba arrived about twenty policemen appeared, stationed at various posts around the prayer hall and at both the main gate and the side gate.

Since it was forbidden to wear shoes in the area immediately surrounding the prayer hall, the policemen walked their posts in bare feet, but they continued to wear their khaki leggings from their ankles to their knees. The rest of their uniform consisted of knee-length, stiffly starched khaki trousers and khaki shirts open at the neck. Some wore red Sam Browne belts and gold cords around their left shoulders.

All of the policemen seemed in awe of Baba and full of respect, both for him and for the pilgrims who had come to see him. When necessary, they always restrained the crowd with a look or a gesture meant to appeal to their sense of reason rather than to intimidate them.

Just as the topic of conversation before Baba arrived had been predominantly concerned with rumors about where he

might be and when he might return, once Baba started selecting people for interviews hardly anyone spoke of anything
other than who got called and what Baba had told them.

Those selected for private interviews would go as whole
family units—wife, children, mother-in-law, nieces, aunts,
cousins, and whoever might have come with the family. He
dealt with each person separately, but none got the same
kind of attention he gave those who came alone.

As soon as a person came out of the room where the private interviews were held, he was surrounded by people unable to contain their curiosity and questioned about the most
minute details of what had taken place. Any evidence that
could even remotely be considered a miracle was seized upon
and circulated throughout the ashram.

Meanwhile, those who had not yet been called for a private interview waited patiently outside the prayer hall, the
women on one side, the men on the other.

Asha was not called the first day, and because she was still
covered with huge welts from the mosquitoes in her room
the night before, she decided not to go back there but to remain outside the prayer hall all night. She was aware that
certain changes were beginning to take place within her, but
she neither questioned nor accepted them, merely noted their
existence and allowed them to happen.

All day the writer circulated among the crowd, listening
to those who had been given private interviews and talking
to as many people as he could.

The tall Brahmin with the English officer's mustache who
cared for the elephant sought the writer out when he heard
he was writing a book. (The elephant had no particular religious or symbolic significance. It was presented to Baba as a
gift of love by an affluent disciple.)

"I was an attorney-at-law," the elephant trainer said. "I
moved in high circles, counting as my closest friends people

like dental surgeons, professional people, but I became accustomed to whisky, having been invited to exclusive clubs, and soon I found myself drinking whisky in the morning and smoking many packets of cigarettes a day until it happened that I no longer could attend to my functions, or what have you, from drinking so much whisky, which was like a curse on me. I couldn't break it. But now I am here, the caretaker of an elephant, and if my friends in Bombay where I come from could see me, oh how they would laugh, but I couldn't think of touching whisky now or cigarettes because Baba has given me such peace. Can you understand this kind of peace? I could never have understood it until I knew it. It would seem I have fallen from the high circles I used to move in, but if I have fallen, I have fallen up, for now I move in the highest of all the possible high circles."

Two men were living in a cave on the nearby hill where Baba used to take his devotees in the old days before he had so many of them. One of the men spoke English, and told the writer that he and his cousin had come to worship Baba and were told to stay in the cave. They had been there two years, the man said, and if it would be possible for the writer to make a small contribution toward their upkeep, the man felt certain that Baba would be pleased.

The writer had already learned about the two men in the cave, and had been warned that they were lying and that Baba had not so much as even seen either one of them, let alone told them to stay in the cave. Nevertheless the story was such a good one and told with such sincerity, he couldn't resist making a small contribution.

He walked through the pilgrims' sheds, watching the huge crows roosting on the naked steel beams, and talked with anyone who would consent to talk with him. There was an almost electric intensity in the air now that Baba was here.

Many people would not talk with anyone about anything. Some were suspicious. Some were superstitious. Some were just unfriendly. Many seemed in a religious trance.

A new rumor had begun circulating. Baba had received a telegram from the pope, it was said, asking if Baba "would grant the pope an interview" on his way to America (a trip Baba had been promising to make for two years). It would require three months' advance notice, however, and the idea that Baba would have to tell anyone where he was going to be three months in advance amused the permanent residents.

"Nobody knows what he's going to do," they said, and they laughed.

In the dirt in front of the prayer hall a yogi, who wore a saffron robe and had shoulder-length hair, sat all day and all night in the full lotus position, never coming out of his deep trance. He seemed to belong to the India of five thousand years ago, except for one detail: he wore sun glasses.

A bus of pilgrims traveling through South India to visit many of the holy places stopped to get permission to see the inside of the prayer hall. They wanted to compare it with the other temples and shrines they had seen. After they had examined it the writer asked them if they were impressed. Baba's temple was somewhat better architecturally than many they had seen, they said, but lower, spiritually.

"In what way?" the writer asked.

"Vibrations," one of them said. The others agreed.

Meanwhile, Surayya and Kasturi were busy from before dawn until late at night carrying messages to and from Baba. If someone wanted a special favor or had come, as one man did, in connection with problems regarding the construction of the college in Bangalore, he first had to find Kasturi, who would inform Baba that the man was here, and then wait for Baba to get an opportunity to see him. In this case the man was granted only two or three minutes, having to follow

Baba and relate the problem to him as Baba walked among the devotees, choosing people for private interviews and, from time to time, distributing *vibhuthi*.

Usually Surayya was the one who summoned the people Baba wanted to see. Being a man of few words, Surayya very seldom would say anything. Instead he would point to the person and motion with his hand for the person to get up and follow him. If the person being called didn't respond quickly enough, Surayya would call after him sharply, "You are wanted!"

It was Surayya who told the doctor to tell the Americans that Baba might see them all together at ten o'clock the next morning. At this point the "Americans" included Steve, Eloise, the writer; the fat businessman whom the writer had seen at Whitefield; his Mexican wife; a student from California, about nineteen; and a sarcastic Australian, about forty-five, who wore a thin beard which looked like continuous sideburns down one side of his face, across his chin, and up the other side of his face.

The Australian and the young man from California had met Baba quite by chance in Madras while Baba was on tour, and for some reason Baba had invited both of them to Bangalore with him and from there on to Puttaparthi. The young American had given himself completely to Baba on sight, being unable even to discuss him without welling up with emotion, but the Australian had not yet made up his mind about anything, really.

"I get along," he said, when asked how he liked India. "I stretch my legs according to the length of the blanket."

"Are you completely dedicated to Baba?" the writer asked.

"I'm not even completely dedicated to life," the Australian said.

They had gathered together that night in the room which

was being shared by the writer, the student, and the Australian. Steve and Eloise had come in to bring some candy they had made from sugar cane Steve had stolen and a coconut he had found, with a few peanuts added, Steve said, to remind him of the only American cultural institution he considered worth saving: The peanut-butter sandwich.

"Did you know that 'loot' was one of the earliest Hindu words to be adopted into the English language?" Steve said in defense of his stolen sugar cane. "It was India, you know, who made England rich enough to be able to afford the luxury of democracy, to beat Napoleon, and to rule the world; that is until they started bringing their fucking women with them wherever they went. You can blame the whole Indian independence thing on your fucking mem-sahibs. They're the ones who brought the stigma of color to India, because the British gentlemen were scared shitless their wives were going to make it with one of the niggers, which they frequently did, by the way."

When the doctor came to tell them they might see Baba in the morning, Steve immediately began threatening what he was going to say and do.

"It's all a question of energy," he said. "The transfer of energy. That's how he makes those things seem to appear in his hand. That's how he reads your mind. But I can meet him head on with just as much energy. Do you realize what the fuck he's doing to these poor people? It's much worse than murder. That only kills the body. This man is fucking around with people's souls."

"If you don't want to go, nobody's making you go," Eloise said.

"You and your going native," he said. "Who do you think you're kidding pretending to be an Indian like a little kid dresses up in her mommy's clothes, going to *bhajans*—all that phony humility and devotion. According to my calculations your state of devotion is only good for about nine hours and then you want to get laid."

The young student didn't want to hear this kind of talk, and, without excusing himself, left the room.

"Have some peanuts," Eloise offered the writer out of embarrassment. "Look how little they are. Not like those gigantic peanuts you get in America with no taste. These little mothers, they've got such a peanut thing happening. Try one."

Steve had compiled a list of questions he was going to ask Baba, but would not reveal what they were. The doctor, laughing, told Steve to make his list carefully because the minute Steve saw Baba's face all of his questions would disappear and he would find himself standing there opening his mouth, but no words would come out.

"Bull shit," Steve said. "It's not every day you get the opportunity to have a meeting with God. I want to find out what death is like, for instance, and why the fuck doesn't he stop the fucking wars. What do we need wars for? And cancer. All he has to do is get a plane-load full of *vibhuthi* and sprinkle it around a little bit." And then, abruptly, he launched into a spaced-out monologue of assorted *non sequiturs*. "You know the best place I ever saw in my whole life? New York City. It was beautiful how hostile everybody was. I didn't want to leave. All you have to do is ask somebody something and they bite your fucking head off. Like I was buying sausages one day and I said to the man how about giving me some big ones, and the man said how about dropping dead? It was beautiful, I was so happy there."

They looked at the ring and the locket Baba had materialized and given to the doctor years ago. Originally it had eight stones, she said, but only half of them were left.

"When I told Baba the stones were falling out," the

doctor explained, "he said that each of those stones stands for one step on the way toward enlightenment, and each time a stone falls out it means I rose up one step. I told him don't give me a ring with such precious stones. My hands are always busy doing things, of course, in water and things like that, but he told me not to tell him what to do. I was getting too big for myself if I now thought he should listen to me." She laughed. "He does that, you know. He knows how to make a joke and put you back where you belong, but he does it with such sweetness you have to laugh."

"I'm not interested in rings or lockets," Steve said. "If he wants to give me something, it's going to have to be much more than dime-store trinkets. I want the truth. The truth! THE TRUTH!" He turned to Eloise. "Come on. Let's go to the room and turn on."

After Steve and Eloise left, the doctor went to the prayer hall, hoping she might get a glimpse of Baba before she went to bed. When she got there she found Asha, who had fallen asleep in the dirt, where she had been sitting all day. The doctor hurried to her room in the hospital and returned with a blanket which she spread over Asha so gently it didn't even awaken her.

Asha didn't wake up until the four o'clock bell rang the next morning, having slept more soundly than she had in months, possibly in years, and without the aid of pills. Automatically she went with the others to the fields, then she followed the woman with the two children to the river, which was only a trickle at that time of year. Asha washed herself in the river, as the others did, feeling a kind of happiness she could not recall ever feeling before.

At about nine-thirty Surayya came hurrying up the stairs of the building where the American group had been waiting together, anxiously, for more than an hour.

"You are wanted!" he said.

Quickly they followed Surayya across the compound to the prayer hall where they passed the envious people waiting and went into a small room at the far end of the building.

The only thing in the room was a life-sized, tinted photograph of Baba in a simple gold frame propped against the wall. As they waited for Baba they looked around the room, noticing *vibhuthi* on the glass covering the picture. Then they arranged themselves in no particular order, taking seats on the floor.

At Puttaparthi Baba began his day at six o'clock in the morning, at which time he would bathe and then, at six-thirty, cross the open balcony from the room in which he lived to the dining room on the other side of the prayer hall. The purpose of the open balcony was to give his devotees an opportunity to take *darsan*, to receive his blessing by seeing him.

In the dining room he had a cup of coffee in a stainless-steel cup with milk and sugar, during which time he discussed the problems of the day with the members of his inner circle. At seven o'clock he came downstairs and walked among the people, selecting thirty or forty of them for private interviews which he would give until nine-thirty. Then he would go back upstairs to the living quarters, wash, again cross the open balcony to the dining room, where he had breakfast, simple South Indian food which was usually cooked by his sister.

Raj Reddy was in charge of looking after Baba's personal comforts and seeing to it that everything functioned properly as far as his living arrangements were concerned.

From ten until eleven, unless special problems arose, Baba would meet foreigners and celebrities of one kind or another who had come, not because of personal problems, but merely to see him. A few minutes after eleven he came downstairs again, as the *bhajans* were sung, and selected another forty or fifty people for private interviews. Occasionally he would stop in the prayer hall and listen to the *bhajans*.

Sometimes he would stand in the doorway for only a moment, at other times he would sit in his special chair, clapping time to the music until the camphor was lighted. On these occasions the camphor was not circulated throughout the room, but offered to him instead.

From twelve until one he took care of the mail, handling about three hundred letters a week.

At one o'clock he ate lunch, and after lunch he would attend to whatever business matters needed attention. Under his immediate control were three colleges, a boys' school, fifteen hundred separate Sathya Sai organizations, the personal problems of millions of devotees, and a highly ambitious program for expansion, including the construction of a library which had already been begun at the ashram, and a number of tours both throughout India and to foreign countries which were in the process of being organized.

At about two-thirty, he usually went to his room and rested until three. Then, after a brief appearance on the balcony, he went to the dining room where he had coffee and discussed business matters for about half an hour, after which he came down and selected more people to be interviewed until six-thirty.

At six-thirty he inspected whatever projects were under construction at the time, visited the school, or saw special groups until it was time for the evening *bhajan* session, which he generally attended. He led the singing in a pure, strong voice, until seven-thirty, at which time he would supervise the meditation, silently correcting the postures of those who needed it.

Dinner was at eight o'clock, after which he would attend

to everything else that needed to be taken care of that day, often working until after midnight.

He was never alone. One or two devotees were selected each night to stay in his room. According to many of them, Baba never slept at all. He would lie on his bed, which also doubled as his couch, and all night long he would explore the air with the fingers of his right hand.

The Americans waited anxiously for Baba to appear. After a few minutes, he came down the stairs from his living quarters, which led directly into the interview room. Steve and Eloise were sitting in the way, not having understood that he would be coming down the steps which were hidden by a curtain. They quickly got up as all of the Americans did, out of respect, Western style, instead of prostrating themselves to touch his feet.

Immediately Baba put them at ease with a warm smile, and gestured that he would sit on the floor against the wall facing the steps and that they should sit on the floor in a semicircle around him.

"Very happy," he said. "Very happy."

The group, waiting for Steve to disrupt the meeting, was somewhat tense. Baba began a general discourse about the importance of having faith in God even though it may be difficult, but Steve neither said nor did anything. He just stared at Baba, not belligerently, but as if he were in a state of semiconsciousness.

"A teacher is like a doctor," Baba said. "He tells you don't eat food you like. Take bitter medicine. Your friend tells you forget about this doctor, enjoy yourself. But who is the friend, your friend or the doctor? But it's very difficult, like doing acrobatics on the edge of a sword over a fire. If you're not careful for one second, *maya* comes in."

Before they realized it, the interview was over. Baba

pushed the sleeve on his right arm over his elbow and holding his fingers apart, his palm down, rotated his hand slowly, closing his fingers. When he opened his fingers he held five aluminum photographs, exactly like the one he had given the writer. He gave one to each of them, skipping the writer.

"You got one," he said.

Then he asked Steve to hold both of his hands together, palms up, the gesture of someone about to receive an offering. When Steve obeyed, Baba made the same rotating motion with his open palm, and when he opened his fingers dozens of tiny pieces of Indian candy, about half an inch long, poured from the center of his palm into both of Steve's hands until they overflowed onto the floor.

"Everybody take some," Baba said. "Candy. It's very delicious Indian candy."

He took the candy which Steve continued to hold in both of his hands and distributed it so that each person got a handful.

"Tomorrow at four o'clock I'll come to your room for private interviews," Baba said.

"Private?" Steve asked.

Baba put his arm on Steve's shoulder and looked very gently into his eyes. "Private. Private."

Baba went upstairs. The group left the room. When they started back toward their living quarters they discovered that each of them had a different idea as to what had taken place.

"Well, you certainly put him in his place," Eloise said to Steve.

Steve looked at her a moment, then he turned and walked away. He went to the top of the hill, outside the compound, where he stayed the rest of the day and night.

The writer went to the shed to see if any of those people he had become acquainted with had been given private

interviews with Baba. As he passed the prayer hall, he saw
the merchant from Ceylon coming out of the interview
room with his wife and children. The merchant was crying.

"This is the happiest moment of my life," he told the
writer. "He gave food to both of my twins. Can you imagine what a blessing that is, to take from the hand of Baba
himself the food for this sacred ceremony? My sons will be
blessed, so blessed, for the rest of their lives."

The tailor was standing in front of the canteen when he
saw the writer. He called to the writer and hurried to him.

"I had my interview," the tailor said. "I had my private
interview."

"What happened?" the writer asked. "What did he say to
you?"

"He was very angry with me," the tailor said. "Before I
said a word I just started to touch his feet, he told me '*bas*,'
which means 'enough,' and he said to me he was so busy
with so much to do, why did I take up his time with business
matters? How could I come to him for money? 'What is
money?' he said. 'I should be worried about money? God is
important, only God, not money.' Well, I didn't know what
to say or what to do, and he said to me, 'Don't worry. I will
give you what you want so go back to your village now.'
Well, I was so surprised I couldn't say anything. I wanted to
say something but I couldn't think of anything to say, but
when I got to the door I realized I couldn't go home. I don't
have enough money to get there. I don't have *any* money.
So I stopped and I started to tell him this, but before I could
say a word he said to me, 'I know, I know. I'll take care of
it,' and then I was outside and I don't know what happened.
I don't know if he said what I thought he said or if he didn't
say it or what he did say. It was all so quick, but I think he
said, 'I'll take care of it.' He said he would take care of it, so

now all I have to do is wait and he will give me the money to get back to my village and everything will be all right."

Because the tailor was one of the few people at the ashram who spoke English fluently, the writer asked if he would be good enough to write to him in America and tell him what happened, to let him know if Baba actually sent the money to him and, if so, how.

The tailor said he would be very happy to do this. Then the writer realized that airmail stamps are very expensive in India, and this man couldn't afford the postage to send a letter to America. So the writer took ten rupees from his pocket and gave them to the tailor.

"You take this," the writer said, "for stamps when you write to me."

The tailor took the money and the writer's address, but he seemed stunned. He stared at the money for a moment and then walked away, as if in a daze.

For a moment the writer couldn't understand what had caused this reaction; then it suddenly occurred to him that he had probably, without knowing it, just given the tailor enough money to get back home. The writer went to the post office and inquired of the clerk how much it would cost to go to the village where the tailor lived.

"Twenty-two rupees," the clerk said.

The writer was puzzled. Obviously, he had not given the tailor enough to get home. He dismissed the matter as unfinished business and continued talking to people in the sheds. About three or four o'clock that afternoon the tailor came running to the writer.

"He sent me the money," the tailor said. "Baba sent Surayya with the money to give me."

"How much did Baba send?" the writer asked.

"Fourteen rupees," the tailor said.

This still didn't add up. If the fare was twenty-two rupees

and the writer had given him ten rupees, the fourteen rupees Baba sent was two rupees too much.

The writer went back to the post office and asked the clerk how long it would take for the tailor to get back to his village.

"Two days," the clerk said.

"How much does it cost, on the average, for a man to feed himself a day?" the writer asked.

"Oh," the clerk said, "about one rupee a day."

The writer found the woman with the two children just as she was about to lie down for her midday nap.

"I heard you got a private interview today," the writer said.

"Yes," she said.

"What did he say?"

"Well, he gave me *vibhuthi* from his hand and he said 'Don't worry, everything will be all right. You are worried about the education of your children,' he said, 'but let me look after them for you.' I asked him, could the boy go to school here because I knew it was only for boys, and he said he wasn't sure. Here they speak only Telugu, and the boy doesn't speak Telugu, he speaks only Hindi. 'But you stay here,' Baba said, 'and I'll ask the teacher.' "

"What about the girl?" the writer asked.

"He didn't say anything specific about the girl."

"Do you feel relieved now that he has told you he will take care of your problems?"

"No," she said, "I don't feel any different. I always knew he would."

"How long will you stay here?"

"Until he tells me to leave," she said.

"Do you have any plans about going back to your village?"

"Plans? Whatever Baba says."

The writer thanked her and before he walked away, she rolled over and seemed already half asleep.

A few minutes later the writer saw Mr. Desai and his son who had polio just as they came from their private interview with Baba.

"He is so wonderful," Desai said. "I can't speak of him without tears coming to my eyes."

"Did he say anything about making the boy walk?"

"Yes. Yes. He said don't worry. He will take care of it, but my son must have more faith, he said, but in time Baba will make him walk, not to worry. 'I promise you,' he said."

The writer turned to the boy. "Do you believe in Baba? Do you think he can make you walk?"

The boy tried to smile, but tears rushed to his eyes. He looked away, to hide the tears, and nodded.

Asha did not get called. She sat all day in front of the prayer hall in the hot sun, and when night came she covered herself with the blanket the doctor had given her and lay down to sleep. She had left the prayer hall only three times, once to buy some fruit in the village, once to get a drink of water at the well, and once to go to the fields. She was no longer waiting, she realized. She was no longer even there.

Steve came down from the hill about three o'clock the next day, but he wouldn't speak to anyone. He sat on the steps of the building where they lived and when everyone saw his troubled look they respected his need to be alone, even Eloise.

The doctor had been supervising the cleaning of the rooms since about noon, having recruited a number of women, permanent residents, to scrub and sweep and tidy up.

"The problem is we don't know which room he will

choose," she said. "You can be sure if we choose one room for him to visit, he will positively choose another one, so they must all be clean. Everything must be perfect."

In one room, the one the doctor hoped Baba would choose, she spread a piece of red silk on a chair for Baba to sit on.

When she brought a basket of raisins, nuts, and dried apricots to put beside Baba's chair, the writer reached for a handful but the doctor quickly stopped him. No one was allowed to touch them until Baba tasted them, she said.

The writer apologized.

"You must love raisins," the doctor said.

"Just the idea of tasting something that isn't going to burn the roof of my mouth off," the writer said.

The doctor laughed. "We like to taste what we eat."

At a few minutes after four Baba could be seen walking across the compound toward the building where the Americans roomed. He was followed by Surayya. The crowd that had gathered around him made way for him to walk through, and then, adhering to some unspoken rule, they stopped following him as he left the area immediately surrounding the prayer hall and just stood there watching him walk away.

"Here he comes! He's coming!" somebody said. The doctor called to Steve, telling him to come up to the porch and wait with everyone else. He got up immediately and joined them.

Nobody, including the doctor, knew exactly what to do.

The one room which had not been cleaned was the one where Steve and Eloise lived. It was obviously too small, the doctor had decided.

Baba stopped a moment to inspect the children chanting Vedas in the shed across from the one where the Americans lived, and then he came up the stairs to the porch where everybody lined up and bowed respectfully, their palms together in front of their faces.

He looked at each of them individually, and then followed the doctor to the room she hoped he would choose for the interview.

"No," he said, without giving any reason.

He walked along the porch and looked at the other rooms, finding each one unsatisfactory.

The maharaja's daughter prostrated herself in front of him and started to touch his feet when he came to her room, but he stopped her, reprimanding her sharply in Hindi for something she had or had not done.

As he turned and started to walk away she said something, her voice trembling, but he gave no indication of having heard her. She stood a moment, watching him, tears in her eyes, then she went into her room and closed the door.

"Open this one," Baba said to Surayya, pointing to the one room that was locked.

Frantically, Surayya tried one key after another but either he did not have the proper key, or, in his confusion, could not find it.

Impatient at Surayya's incompetence, Baba walked to the end of the building and looked into the room where Steve and Eloise lived.

"All right, this one," he said.

There was a great deal of confusion as all of those in the American group tried to seat themselves in the tiny, cluttered room. No one knew quite where to sit, waiting until Baba had first taken his seat, but for a moment he just stood there, looking around the room at the air mattress under the cot, at the fruit and vegetables on the floor.

The doctor found a straw mat under some pots and placed it against one wall after moving the luggage and books and guitar out of the way.

Baba continued to stand there a moment, looking at them all with disapproval, then he sat on the mat. The others spaced themselves as well as they could around him.

When Eloise started to sit between Steve and the businessman, Steve shouted at her.

"Not over here, dummy! Women over there!"

Eloise got up and joined the Mexican wife of the businessman. The doctor discreetly left the room.

"Well," Eloise said, "at last."

"What?" Baba asked.

"At last we got settled," Eloise said.

"Jesus Christ!" Steve said to Eloise. "Why don't you grow up, for Christ's sakes?"

There was an awkward silence. Baba seemed to be growing more displeased. He sat a moment, exploring the air with the fingers of his right hand.

Suddenly Steve started talking. It was as if all of the questions he had been storing up since he came to the ashram had suddenly exploded, involuntarily bursting out of his mouth like a series of firecrackers.

"What should a disciple do? Meditate? Pray? What is death? Is there any one thing to know in order to know it all? How can I control my mind? How can I keep my thoughts from driving me crazy?"

"Sit in light," Baba said. "The light in you. You are the light."

"How can I control my mind?" Steve asked. "If I could just control my mind!"

"Meditate," Baba said. "Concentrate on breathing in one nostril and out the other, then the mind's attention flows and it keeps your thoughts from wandering. Later, choose one point of God to meditate on." He looked at the writer. "In America you have your air-conditioned rooms, but where is your mental peace? What good is sitting in air-conditioned rooms if your mind is in hell? In India we have no air conditioning but we know peace. God."

"Some people in America know it," the writer said. "Some people in India don't."

"But what if your mind is cunning and evil and tells you to do terrible things?" Steve asked.

"What?" Baba asked.

"He doesn't understand Krishnamurti," Eloise said.

"Will you just shut up?" Steve said. "Why don't you shut up?"

"Sit up straight!" Baba said to Eloise, who had stretched her legs out.

"There's not too much room in here, you know," Eloise said.

The others in the room, except for Baba and Steve, laughed.

"Quiet!" Baba said. "Prasanthi Nilayam means perfect peace, a peaceful place."

"Pearls before swine," Steve said.

"You take care of your pearls," Eloise said, "I'll take care of mine."

Steve turned away from her, making a point of ignoring her.

"You say you are Shirdi," Steve said to Baba. "He died eight years before you were born. Where were you those eight years?"

"What?" Baba said, not understanding the question.

"For eight years," Steve explained, "you were not on this earth. Where were you? In heaven? What is heaven? Were you dead? What is death?"

"Samadhi," Baba said. "You know this word?"

"Yes," Steve said, "but what is it like there?"

Abruptly, Baba got up. He pointed to Steve and motioned for him to come with Baba into the other room. Steve followed him immediately.

"What do you want?" Baba was heard to ask.

"I can't answer that," Steve said. "It's too difficult."

"No, no," Baba said. "Material things. What can I give you?"

"I don't want anything material," Steve said. "I don't like rings. I never wear a ring. I want the truth. I want peace. I want will power."

There was a long pause. Those in the other room could hear Baba whispering, but they couldn't hear what he said. In a moment, when Steve came out, he was ashen.

On the afternoon of the fourth day Asha was finally selected by Baba for an interview. She went into the room at the prayer hall with about twenty other people and sat there waiting as he appeared from behind the curtain in front of the steps and pointed first to one person, then another who joined him on the steps behind the curtain, then after their interview, left. After about ten people had been called, Baba pointed to Asha. She got up and went to join him behind the curtain. Without realizing it she was crying.

"Don't cry," Baba said before she had a chance to say a word. "I will cure your husband's cancer."

He made the rotating motion with his open palm and transferred a handful of *vibhuthi* from his hand to hers.

At precisely the moment Baba gave her the ashes her husband sat up in bed, over eleven hundred miles away, and spoke for the first time in two weeks.

"I can hear," he said.

☙ TWELVE

The writer left Tokyo at two forty-five in the afternoon and arrived the same day in Los Angeles a few minutes before ten in the morning, nearly five hours before he left. This footnote was numbly added to the glob of disturbing impressions searching for a home in his brain. He had planned a two- or three-day stopover in Tokyo on his way back to America to give him an opportunity to regain a perspective, but not even the Japanese baths could help him make the transition from the timeless irreality of India to goal-oriented America.

After six weeks in Baba's murky world, neither the word Reality nor the word Illusion seemed to fit any familiar definition. Was a dream not real? Even an unreal dream, if there could be such a thing, would be a real, unreal dream, just as, for example, being sentenced to a life as a pneumatic drill operator five days a week in a city like New York seemed to the writer to be far more nightmarish than a sleeper's endless fall through space or the familiar dream of running for one's life from some known or unnamed terror, the breath pounding, the legs pumping, but with no forward motion whatsoever.

Ultimately, though, what was it all about but words? If the true core of the soul can be found only in the Absolute, suppose one could by perseverance or by chance actually crash through the mirror image of the Self and find somewhere in the infinity of inner space the *"Real* Self"? The Self would know it was the Self. What need could it have to be defined, either as Illusion or Reality or, the writer reluctantly added, as "Truth"?

For six weeks the writer had struggled to find his equilibrium in the extra-dimensional India of which he himself had been a part. The seventh week, the real (or unreal) world of his pre-Baba personality began to infiltrate. His agent in Hollywood managed to reach him with a cablegram, which had been transmitted in India from city to town to village to wilderness until it finally arrived in Puttaparthi in Morse code. By the time the message was delivered into the hands of the writer, it had been thoroughly anagrammatized by a series of well-meaning but baffled telegraphers, none of whom apparently had even the most rudimentary knowledge of the English language. After a while the writer was able to decode the essence of the message: it was imperative that he go to Hollywood at once. Then came a barrage of anxious cablegrams from his business manager in New York, most of which proved to be equally indecipherable, but the tone of urgency was unmistakable. Decisions had to be made in connection with negotiations under way for future film projects. The outcome of an income tax audit needed immediate approval.

The writer tried to cable his decisions, but days later, when the confusing answers to his answers came back, it became clear that it was impossible to maintain any kind of coherent dialogue between Puttaparthi and New York or Hollywood.

Sitting on top of the high rock overlooking the ashram, he wore an inexpensive, knee-length, white silk *kurta* over his tight-legged white broadcloth jodhpurs (a manner of dress more common in the cities of the North than the villages of the South). The black dye from the sandals he had bought his first day in India had penetrated the soles of his feet so deeply no amount of scrubbing had been able to wash it off. The first few nights at the ashram he had tried to wash his feet before crawling under the mosquito net onto the thin, army-style mattress the doctor had appropriated for him; but after a while he stopped noticing his black-bottomed feet. He also stopped combing his hair the way he usually did.

For several years, since he had lost most of the hair on the top of his head, he had let the hair on the left side grow almost shoulder length so that with patient fluffing, meticulous arranging, and an abundance of hair spray it would make what he knew was a ludicrous attempt to cover the baldness. He could not remember the exact rationalization he had used to persuade his usually fanatic sense of honesty to permit this transparent nondeception. Even now when he saw a man with hair combed exactly like his own, his first reaction was one of amusement, if not affectionate pity, but this was quickly followed by the harsh voice of the conscience of his conscience. Like an old-fashioned Hollywood gangster, his Super Ego invariably burst into his consciousness to sentence his defenseless Ego to a few minutes of brutal lacerations. It occurred to him that perhaps the punishment was the real prize his Ego was after and that was why he wore his hair as he did. On the other hand, the picture of himself as a short, fat, balding Jew so violated his secret image of himself as Cary Grant that it would not be too difficult for him to clutch at the shadow of any deception if only it could narrow by even a millimeter the light years between how he actually looked and how he allowed himself to feel he looked.

After the first two or three days at the ashram, however,

he found himself letting his hair be his hair for what it was and nothing more. His bald spot was his bald spot. He stopped trying to hide it, combing the hair on both sides straight down the sides of his head instead of spreading the left side over the top. Inasmuch as the hair on his left side reached to his shoulder and the hair on the right was more or less normal length, it made him look like half a hippie, which perhaps he indeed was, he decided.

He wanted to believe this newly found lack of pretense symbolized some kind of sudden contact with the Real Self, reflecting an affinity, finally, with the Absolute, but he had to admit that it also was just too goddamned much trouble to bother with hair at a place like Puttaparthi, and having conceded that, he was forced to consider the possibility that what he hoped might be a beautiful breakthrough into the Universal Life Force might instead be nothing more than a snob's contempt for the people around him. There was no need to impress either Sai Baba or any of his devotees. So why bother?

The moment of truth would come, he knew, the day he returned to what he still considered "civilization."

For a time he sat on the rock and listened to the devotees in the prayer hall some distance below sing their morning heartaches to their saviour, who, they prayed, would take away their suffering. In the soft light filtered by the myopia the writer had learned to live with without glasses, the ashram looked like a pastel water color which had been smudged before it had dried. He looked through the half dozen cablegrams he had brought with him to evaluate in privacy on the rock, and then, presently, he got up and started back toward the compound. He no longer looked in terror for snakes at every step as he had done when he first arrived at Puttaparthi. Not that he had acquired anything like a warm feeling for cobras. He simply had grown more relaxed, and like it or not, he had to acknowledge the fact.

Inside the compound he stopped to sit on the steps of the building where he lived. He thought about his situation carefully and then he wrote a note asking Baba for permission to leave the next day and requesting a few minutes of his time in private, if possible, before he left. He took the note to Kasturi, who promised to deliver it at the first opportunity.

The next day Surayya found the writer in the pilgrims' open shed and motioned for him to hurry.

"You are wanted!" Surayya said.

The writer quickly followed Surayya upstairs over the prayer hall to Baba's living quarters. Surayya did not go into the room. After ushering the writer in from the stairway, he hurried back down the steps to carry out his next order of business.

Baba was on the thin mattress supported by a simple frame and four wooden legs which served both as a studio couch during the day and as his bed at night. He was leaning against a few small pillows propped against the wall. Before he looked up to note the writer's arrival he continued to go through his mail, looking at each letter, still unopened and in its envelope, until a thought formed in his head, then he put it on top of the stack of letters on the couch to the left of him before reaching to take another letter from the stack on the couch to the right of him. After a minute or two he looked up and smiled at the writer.

"Come in," he said. "Come in."

The writer stepped into the room and bowed slightly, both palms together on his chest just under his chin.

"So," Baba said. He paused to look directly into the writer's eyes. "So, you have seen enough."

"Too much. I don't understand anything I've seen."

Baba laughed.

"Appearance is not different from emptiness," Baba said struggling for the words in English. "Yet within emptiness there is no appearance."

The writer felt he should smile or nod or indicate in some way that he understood what Baba had said, but he did not understand and he resisted the temptation to pretend that he did.

Baba nodded. "Life is only the memory of a dream," he said. "It comes from no visible rain. It falls into no recognizable sea. Some day, not for a while yet, you will understand how meaningless it is to spend your whole life trying to accumulate material things. I have no land, no property of my own where I can grow my own food. Everything is registered in the name of someone else, but just as those people in the village who have no land wait until the pond dries up so they can scratch the land with a plow and quickly grow something before the pond fills up again, I grow my food which is joy or love. To you the words have different meanings, but to me both words are the same. But I have to do it quickly, quickly in the hearts of those who come to see me, quickly before they leave."

He looked up again into the writer's eyes.

"The kind of belief in me I ask of people is more, much more than most people think is faith or love," Baba said. "That's why many people who come just to see the miracles stop loving me the minute I stop entertaining them and giving them presents. No. What I ask you to do is give me everything. Not fruit or flowers or money or land, but *you*, all of you with nothing held back. Your mind. Your heart. Your soul . . ." He stopped and paused, then nodded to himself. "But those are just words."

They were silent for a time.

The writer stood beside the couch and waited. There was

nothing he could say. A kind of warmth and closeness he
had never known before was spreading through his consciousness and it frightened him. He felt in danger of being
smothered by it, but it wasn't just the intensity of the feeling that disturbed him. It was the sudden realization that this
feeling of love—he *thought* it was love—was different from
any other kind of love he had ever felt or heard about or
read of before. It may have been this inability to define what
he felt that caused him suddenly to panic. In less than a
minute he had become a displaced person, emotionally, isolated in the dark unknown, and to cope with this puzzling
anxiety the only defense he could find was to try to turn it
off.

Baba watched him for a time with intensity.

"You cannot run away from me," Baba said. "As I told
you, no one can come to Puttaparthi, however accidental it
might seem, without my calling him. I bring only those people here who are ready to see me, and nobody else, nobody,
can find his way here. When I say 'ready' there are different
levels of readiness, you understand."

Baba laughed. "You wonder why I called you here instead
of millions of other people because you don't like the way
you feel for me. Isn't it? And it makes you worry why I
called you."

The writer laughed, his tension broken, and Baba laughed
with him.

"It worries me," the writer said. "When you ask me to
give myself to you completely. I can't do that. I spent too
long getting control of my life to just blindly become somebody's slave, even if you're God, or not God, just a man with
superhuman powers of yoga. I don't trust anybody that
much."

"Do you trust yourself?" Baba asked.

The writer smiled. "Not much."

"I know your past and I know your future so I know why you suffer and how you can escape suffering and when you finally will."

"When I die?" The writer was being half-facetious.

"Yes, I know," Baba said. "In all your past lives too, you were always afraid of death."

"I'm not afraid of death."

"That's all you are afraid of," Baba said. "You think death is something bad, but death is neither bad nor good. Death is death."

"What purpose does it serve?"

"Why does a person die?" Baba took a moment to reflect. He looked at his fingers. "So he won't die again. He is born so he won't be born again."

"I don't understand," the writer said.

"Life is only relatively real," Baba said. "Until death it only appears to be real. And, after all, the only part that dies is the body, not the person who lives in the body. When a cat or a dog dies he leaves the world the same as before he lived in it, but a man should leave the world a better place than when he came into it. For no other reason was he born, for no other reason does he die."

"Are you God?" The writer heard himself say. He had not planned to go into that subject at all.

"Why do you waste your time and energy trying to explain me?" Baba said, with a trace of irritation. "Can a fish measure the sky? If I had come as Narayana with four arms they would have put me in a circus, charging money for people to see me. If I had come only as a man, like every other man, who would listen to me? So I had to come in this human form, but with more than human powers and . . ." he groped for the word, "wisdom."

"Then you *are* God. Is that what you're saying?"

"First you have to understand yourself. I told you that.

And then you will understand me. I'm not a man, I'm not a woman. I'm not old. I'm not young. I'm all of these."

The writer laughed, without quite knowing why. He was embarrassed for having asked the question and unnerved by the answer. Here was a human being, or what looked like one, curled up on a studio couch, his legs tucked beneath him like a teen-age girl, and there was nothing the writer could think of that would allow him to accept the idea that this person with the Afro hairdo and the orange dress could actually, literally, be God.

"Some people think it's a beautiful thing," Baba said, "for the Lord to be on the earth in human form, but if you were in my place you would not feel it's so beautiful. I know everything that happened to everybody in the past, present, and future, so I'm not so quick to give people the mercy they beg me for. I know why a person has to suffer in this life and what will happen to him the next time he's born because of that suffering this time, so I can't act the way people want me to. They call me cold-hearted one time, soft-hearted the next. Why don't I do this? Why don't I do that? Why don't I stop all wars forever and get rid of all disease and suffering? What they don't know is I'm not responsible for suffering. I don't cause suffering any more than I cause happiness and joy. People make their own palaces and their own chains and their own prisons."

"Can I write about that in my book?" the writer asked.

"What do you know about me?" Baba asked. "Do you believe in me the way I said you have to believe in me?"

"Not yet."

"Then how can you write about me? You're like a child. When I give you what you want or make you laugh, you love me, but the next minute when I'm too busy and can't see you the minute you want me to, you want to kill me. Isn't it? You listen to me with respect, but then in private you laugh at me. What kind of book can you possibly write about me?"

"That kind of book. Exactly."

"For what purpose? Publicity? I don't need publicity. I'm not your Mahesh Yogi, don't forget, on television with the singers."

"What are you telling me? I can't write the book?"

Baba laughed. "Write it. Write your book. That's your duty, your *dharma*. But write the truth. Only what you saw here. Only the truth. How you laughed at me, hated me, that's part of it; and if you want to, how you loved me, the few times you let yourself love me."

Baba took both of his hands and rubbed them as hard as he could on the writer's chest, massaging it vigorously as if to stimulate the writer's spiritual circulation.

"I am always with you," Baba said. "Even when you don't believe in me, even when you try to forget me. Even when you laugh at me or hate me. Even when I seem to be on the opposite side of the earth. But you need material things to remind you, isn't it?"

He pushed up his sleeve and rotated his open palm as he closed his fingers. When he opened them he was holding a gold ring with his picture painted on porcelain in the center, surrounded by sixteen stones which seemed to be diamonds. He put the ring on the writer's finger. It fit perfectly.

The writer laughed. "How can I ever get this through customs?"

"Don't worry," Baba said. "I'll take care of it."

He touched the ring with his fingertips.

"I am in you," Baba said. "You are in me. Don't forget that. We cannot be separated."

Once having made the decision to go, the writer was eager to leave. He called a taxi from Bangalore and spent the rest of the day until it arrived distributing all of the unused supplies he had brought with him. Without exception, all of the older people he approached politely refused anything he offered them. They had everything they wanted in Baba. It was only the younger devotees and the American visitors who eagerly accepted his aspirins, Alka Seltzer, ball-point pens, and special, melt-proof tropical Hershey bars.

He looked everywhere for the doctor. Of all the people at the ashram she was the one he felt the closest to, and the person he would most likely miss. He hated the idea of having to leave without saying good-by to her, but finally, influenced by the driver's revelation that the headlights on the taxi were not working too well (freely translated, "not at all"), the writer left her a note and started down the steps toward the car. Just as he got to the taxi he heard something behind him and turned to see the doctor racing down the steep rock stairs from the hospital on top of the hill. He ran to meet her but when they met they both stopped for an instant, neither knowing quite what to do. To kiss would have been inappropriate—although that seemed to be the impulse both of them barely managed to suppress. Instead, the writer smiled and touched her hand.

"Here," she said, relying on the safety of her gruffness. "Something to eat on the way."

She gave him a silk handkerchief tied around the raisins and nuts she had prevented him from eating when Baba had come to the American quarters. Then she took something else from her cloth bag and put it into his hand.

He didn't immediately know what it was, but then he remembered that once he had casually mentioned an ancient palm leaf with a poem written on it that he had seen in New Delhi but didn't buy because it was too expensive.

"It's only five or six hundred years old," the doctor said. "That's a prescription written on it. That's the way they used to do it then."

"I can't accept this," the writer said. "It's very valuable."

"Why should I give you something not valuable?" she said.

They said good-by and she stood watching the car drive out of the compound and onto the dirt path which within a few hundred yards would disintegrate into no path at all.

In the car, the driver could hardly contain himself. "I saw him," the driver told the writer excitedly. "I touched Baba's feet. While I was waiting for you I saw all these people and I went to see what was taking place and he was there and he came just to me and I touched his feet. This morning I knew it would be an auspicious day. I saw a bird before breakfast. I didn't even want to go to work today, but one of the drivers had a traffic accident so the owner sent a small boy to fetch me and just as I arrived, that very moment, your call came through so he turned to me since I was standing there and told me to go and get you. If I had arrived five minutes later or came to work when I was supposed to, it wouldn't have happened."

Unconsciously, the writer plowed his fingers through his hair, and only after he had begun to do it did he realize that what he was doing was spreading the hair over his bald spot.

On the flight across the Pacific it seemed to the writer as if he had been gone at least as long as Rip Van Winkle, but within two hours after he had checked into the Beverly Hills Hotel it was hard to remember he had been away. The doorman, half a dozen bellmen, the room clerk, the maid on the floor all greeted him warmly and by name as if they had seen him only the day before. His usual suite with the fireplace and the patio was waiting for him, with the basket of fruit on the coffee table, one gigantic vase of flowers in its usual place on top of the color-television set in the sitting room and another one on the dresser in the bedroom.

Lunch with his agent at the swimming pool was exactly like every other lunch he had eaten there, with all the lusciously breasted starlets on display ignoring the magnificent studs on display to concentrate on one or a number of fat-bellied promoters who might be helpful to their careers.

Nothing had changed.

"How was India?" the agent asked, without wanting to know. "Did you get laid?"

The writer knew better than to try to discuss any part of the experience seriously, but even as he related the most superficial account, purely in the interest of convention, he knew the agent was only barely pretending to listen.

The ring Baba had given the writer held the agent's attention for a moment.

"No shit," the agent said when the writer told of how Baba had materialized it out of the air, but it was obvious that in that fraction of a second the agent had immediately categorized Baba as just another magic act, and, as such, virtually unbookable except maybe once on the Sullivan show.

That night the writer had dinner alone in his room. He had called his family that morning as soon as he got to the hotel. He had called from Tokyo to tell them he was on his way back, but that call was mainly to reassure himself that his family was safe from all the catastrophes he had imagined. Every time he took a trip anywhere alone he always expected to come back and find his house burned down, his wife and children slaughtered by a madman. This call was to communicate with his family, but whatever it was he had hoped the conversation might be, it wasn't. The children had the flu, the cleaning woman had disappeared with a hundred dollars and two of his wife's dresses. Otherwise they were fine. Everything was the same. They all missed him and were glad he was back, but there was no way to convey to them where he had been emotionally. Not that he had the vaguest idea himself.

And so instead of calling his wife again and burdening her

with his childish need to summarize, he sat at the flimsy room-service table, lingering over his wine and trying without too much success to attribute the vague uneasiness he felt to the jet lag instead of to his gnawing ambivalence. He had no intention of giving up the luxuries of life. Not willingly. And yet, finding himself suddenly back in a world where relationships were not formed but negotiated, he knew there had to be some middle land somewhere between Beverly Hills and Puttaparthi. More than anything at the moment he wanted to talk about it, but there was no one he could think of who would listen except out of love or politeness, and that, of course, would defeat the purpose.

He looked at the ring Baba had given him, which now seemed to be the only tangible proof he had that he had actually been away. Going through customs at San Francisco he had made a point of calling the ring to the attention of the inspector.

"I don't know how much it's worth," he said. "It was a gift. But I'm sure it's real and I want to pay the duty on it."

The inspector studied the ring carefully, then gave it to another inspector to look at. They both agreed the ring was worthless.

A few days later, though, when he returned to New York, he called the Metropolitan Museum of Art to ask for the name of the most reliable jewelry appraisers they could recommend. On their recommendation, he took the ring to the Commonwealth Appraisal Corporation, where the ring was described as: "Lady's 18K gold and white sapphire ring, oval top circled with sixteen faceted white sapphires, total weight approximately 2.40 carats, center set with oval cloisonné enamel depicting a dignitary seated in a chair. Value: $125.00."

He framed two large color photographs of Baba and hung

them in his office. For weeks he examined them several times a day to see if any *vibhuthi* had formed on the glass, but there was no sign of anything resembling ashes—either holy or otherwise.

Several months after he returned he had a dream he considered worth recording. That day he had been searching for a folder which contained some business correspondence he urgently needed. If he didn't find a particular letter in the folder it would cost him a great deal of money.

Both the writer and his secretary had looked in every conceivable corner, but finally they had had to give up. That night, in the dream, he saw Baba open a specific drawer in a filing cabinet used only for manuscripts in dead storage. In the middle of the drawer was the folder the writer needed.

The next morning the writer looked in that drawer and found the folder exactly where Baba had found it in the dream.

One day, motivated by what he considered the most practical of reasons, he stopped wearing the ring Baba had given him. It was too fragile, he decided, and too gaudy, and he found it much too boring to constantly keep explaining how he got it and why he wore it.

Months later a letter arrived from a friend in New Delhi. Among other items of interest he wrote news of Asha. When she had returned to New Delhi from Puttaparthi she followed Baba's instructions and gave her husband a pinch of *vibhuthi* in water once a day for three days. Within five weeks he was completely cured and back at his desk, in the office adjoining the writer's friend. Now, a year and a half later, the writer's friend wrote, Asha's husband had been hospitalized for cancer of the lungs.

Asha did not go to see Baba this time. Three months later her husband died.